Legal Aspects of Financial Services Regulation and the Concept of a Unified Regulator

The George
and Helen
Ladd Library

Law, Justice, and Development

The Law, Justice, and Development series is offered by the Legal Vice Presidency of the World Bank to provide insights into aspects of law and justice that are relevant to the development process. Works in the series present new legal and judicial reform activities related to the World Bank's work, as well as analyses of domestic and international law. The series is intended to be accessible to a broad audience as well as to legal practitioners.

Series Editor: Salman M. A. Salman
Editorial Board: Dominique Bichara, Hassane Cisse, Alberto Ninio, Kishor Uprety

Legal Aspects of Financial Services Regulation and the Concept of a Unified Regulator

Kenneth Kaoma Mwenda
Senior Counsel
Legal Vice Presidency
The World Bank

THE WORLD BANK
Washington, D.C.

ISBN-10: 0-8213-6459-6   eISBN: 0-8213-6460-X
ISBN-13: 978-0-8213-6459-8   DOI: 10.1596/978-0-8213-6459-8

Library of Congress Cataloging-in-Publication Data
Mwenda, Kenneth Kaoma.
    Legal aspects of financial services regulation and the concept of a unified regulator /
Kenneth Koama Mwenda
        p. cm — (Law, justice, and development)
    Includes bibliographical references and index.
    ISBN-13: 978-0-8213-6459-8
    ISBN-10: 0-8213-6459-6
        1. Financial institutions—Law and legislation. 2. Administrative law. 3. Banks and
banking—State supervision. I. Title. II. Series.

K1066.M945 2006
346.73'082—dc22
                                                                2005057741

Contents

List of Tables and Figures

Foreword

Over the years, financial regulation and supervision in many countries has been organized around specialist agencies that have distinct and separate responsibilities for banking, securities, and insurance. In recent years, however, there has been an emerging trend in some countries towards restructuring the financial supervisory function, and in particular creating unified regulatory agencies (agencies that supervise two or more of these areas). The fact that a number of countries are now moving towards integrating the different supervisory functions into a single agency, and that different types of financial services and products continue to spring up in the financial sector of many countries, are indications of the changing global landscape of the financial services industry. Equally important as indicators of the evolving course of financial services regulation are increases in the number of countries where universal banking is practiced and in the numbers of parent and subsidiary companies providing different types of financial services and products.

This study examines the policy bases of different countries adopting various regulatory and institutional models of unified financial services supervision and addresses some of the key characteristics of these models. The study also highlights the progress achieved by the unified regulators in adopting a consistent framework for the regulation and supervision of all financial intermediaries they oversee. Practical problems faced by countries in setting up unified regulators are identified, and the study highlights important legal and policy issues that should be considered when developing regulatory and institutional models of unified financial services supervision.

The Legal Vice Presidency is pleased to offer this publication and hopes that it will provide better understanding of financial services regulation and, more generally, of the relationship between law and financial sector development.

Roberto Dañino
Senior Vice President and General Counsel
The World Bank

September 2005

Abstract

This study deals with legal and policy issues underpinning the development and strengthening of the regulatory and institutional framework for unified financial services supervision. The study discusses developments in a number of jurisdictions, among them Australia, Canada, Estonia, Germany, Hungary, Ireland, Latvia, Malta, the Scandinavian countries, the United Kingdom, and the United States.

Chapter 1 examines conceptual issues to be taken into account in designing a sound regulatory and institutional framework for financial services supervision. The chapter also provides a working definition of "regulation" and delves into the intricacies of designing the appropriate regulatory framework. Chapter 2 analyzes the concept of an independent financial services regulator, arguing that a unified regulator that is both independent and accountable would help promote the development of a sound financial sector. Chapter 3 discusses the concept of a unified regulator, examining the question of whether every country should adopt a model of unified financial services supervision. Chapter 4 provides country studies, addressing the efficacy of the framework for unified financial services supervision in Latvia, the United Kingdom, and the Scandinavian countries. Finally, Chapter 5 spells out policy recommendations and possible constitutional and legal challenges that might be encountered when a country is considering unifying its regulation of financial services.

Acknowledgements

I would like to extend my thanks and appreciation to colleagues who served as reviewers of this book: Gerry N. Muuka, Professor and Assistant Dean of the Business School, Murray State University, Kentucky, USA; Jose De Luna Martinez, Senior Financial Economist, Financial Sector Operations and Policy Unit, World Bank; and Peter R. Kyle and Nagavalli Annamalai, both Lead Counsels, Financial, Private Sector and Infrastructure Development Practice Group (LEGPS), Legal Vice Presidency, World Bank. I am grateful to all of them for their insightful and valuable comments on the earlier drafts of this book.

My thanks also go to World Bank colleagues Roberto Dañino, Senior Vice President and General Counsel; David Freestone, Deputy-General Counsel (Advisory Practice Groups); Elizabeth Adu, Deputy-General Counsel (Operational Practice Groups); Salman M. A. Salman, Lead Counsel, Environmental and Socially Sustainable Development and International Law (LEGEN); and Vijay S. Tata, Chief Counsel, LEGPS, for the support rendered toward the publication of this book. Further, my thanks go out to Alex E. Fleming, my former manager at the World Bank, for raising an intellectual curiosity in me on important aspects of unified financial services supervision, and to Shéhan de Sayrah, Counsel, LEGEN, for his editorial assistance.

And I cannot stop without thanking my many good friends and family members, including professional colleagues, whose names, if I were to list them all, would occupy a whole chapter in this book. I thank them all for their support over the years.

Acronyms and Abbreviations

APRA	Australian Prudential Regulatory Authority
ASIC	Australian Securities and Investment Commission
BOJ	Bank of Jamaica
BOZ	Central Bank of Zambia
CAD	Capital Adequacy Directive
CFTC	Commodity Futures Trading Commission
CIS	Commonwealth of Independent States
EU	European Union
FATF	Financial Action Task Force
FSA	Financial Services Authority
FSC	Financial Supervisory Commission
FSMC	Financial Services and Markets Compensation Scheme
FSS	Financial Supervisory Services
GDP	gross domestic product
IMF	International Monetary Fund
MPC	Monetary Policy Committee
OECD	Organisation for Economic Co-operation and Development
OSFI	Office of the Superintendent of Financial Institutions
PIA	Pensions and Insurance Authority
ROCHs	Recognized Overseas Clearing Houses
ROIEs	Recognized Overseas Investment Exchanges
SEC	Securities and Exchange Commission
SFC	Securities and Futures Commission
SROs	self-regulatory organizations

CHAPTER 1

Designing a Sound Regulatory Framework for Financial Services Supervision

1.1 Introduction

There is a noticeable dearth of literature for lawyers and law reform institutions on how to structure, or what to consider when setting up, a unified financial services regulator.[1] While economists have been quick to put pen to paper on both collateral and substantive issues relating to the topic,[2] not much has been written by legal scholars. This book endeavors to fill that gap. The book closes the divide between law and economics on the topic of a unified financial services regulator and provides an interdisciplinary exposition of the law. The book fleshes out practical legal and policy issues to be considered when a sound regulatory and institutional framework is being set up for supervision of financial services.

A central thesis of the book is that until there is a longer track record of experience with unified regulators, it is difficult to come to firm conclusions about the restructuring process itself and the optimal internal structure of such agencies. Underscoring this thesis is the view that there is hardly any evidence of broadly accepted standards of best practices for structuring unified financial services supervision. The design of a regulatory model of unified financial services supervision has in many cases been driven by country-specific conditions and a desire

---

[1] On the concept of a unified financial services regulator, *see generally*, K. K. Mwenda & A. Fleming, *International Developments in the Organizational Structure of Financial Services Supervision: Part I*, 16(12) J. Intl. Banking L. 291–298 (2001) (hereafter *International Developments Part I*); and K. K. Mwenda & A Fleming, *International* 7–18 (2002) (hereafter *International Developments Part II*). *See also* K. K. Mwenda, *Integrated Financial Services Supervision in Poland, the UK and the Nordic Countries,* 10(2) Tilburg For. L. Rev. 144–168 (2002); E. Ferran, *Examining the UK's Experience in Adopting a Single Financial Regulator Model,* 28 Brook. J. Intl. L. 257 (2003), http://islandia.law. yale.edu/ccl/papers/symposium10-21-03/2-4Panel2Ferransingleregulator.pdf (accessed May 25, 2004); and E. Daemestri & F. Guerrero, *The Rationale for Integrated Financial Services Supervision in Latin America and the Caribbean,* Sustainable Development Department Technical Paper Series; IFM-135 (Inter-American Development Bank 2003), http://www.iadb.org/sds/doc/IFM-2003-135-Integrating_Financial_Sup-E.pdf (accessed May 25, 2004).

[2] This view is evident from the increasing amount of literature that is being churned out by economists—most of that work is referenced in this book—on the topic of a unified financial services regulator.

by some countries to adopt what appear to be current international trends in models of financial sector regulation.

To encourage a better understanding of how to structure an efficient and effective regulatory and institutional framework for supervision of more than one segment of financial services, the book begins by examining the basis for and objectives of financial services regulation, highlighting the different roles regulators must play. This analysis is designed to provide the reader with a conceptual framework to underpin the central thesis of the study. A discussion of the enforcement powers of a regulator, and an analysis of whether or not the regulator follows a rules-based model, is based on government policies for introducing a unified regulator. The closely related discussion of the disparities in organizational structure and unified regulatory frameworks in different countries demonstrates the absence of best practices in this field.

Against this backdrop, Chapter 1 sets in context the conceptual and theoretical framework underpinning the thesis, highlighting the historical development of the concept of a unified financial services regulator. An examination of the critical issues in establishing a sound framework for the supervision of financial services is laid out here. The chapter first introduces the main thesis before examining the jurisprudence of financial sector regulation. The jurisprudential analysis covers the concept of financial sector regulation, the objectives of regulation, the design of a regulatory framework, models of financial sector regulation in Europe and other parts of the world, and the constituent elements of a sound regulatory framework.

Building on Chapter 1, Chapter 2 examines the concept of an independent regulator as a corollary to an efficient and effective framework for financial services supervision. The thesis is advanced that, although the concept of an independent regulator provides incentives for regulators and supervisors to do quality work, the independence of a regulator may not necessarily prevent the occurrence of a financial crisis. The crux of the matter, it is argued, lies in recognizing that achieving both political independence and independence from the industry regulated is as important as ensuring that the independent regulator is accountable.

After Chapter 3 introduces the concept of a unified financial services regulator, explaining the difference between a *partially* and a *fully* unified regulator and fleshing out the obstacles and challenges different countries have faced in implementing models of unified financial services regulation. It then examines issues and themes in the contemporary debate on unified financial services supervision. Chapter 4 places that discussion in context by examining models of unified financial services regulators in Latvia, Norway, Denmark, Sweden, and the United Kingdom. However, before examining the regulatory environment in these countries, it is important to first understand that the financial services industry to be regulated is diverse. Therefore, the structure of the regulatory and institutional framework in every country will depend in part on the objectives of regulation and the size of the financial sector. Further, the type of risk control systems in place and the effectiveness of these systems can affect the structure of the regulatory and institutional framework. As the International Compliance Association observes:

> [The financial services industry] operates on numerous different levels and can be divided and subdivided in various ways. Different countries have their own financial services industries, which are comprised of different market sectors, providing various forms of service in relation to different forms of product. Even though economic liberalisation during the twentieth century has caused an unprecedented level of cohesion amongst these national financial systems—to the extent that there now exists a single global financial marketplace—that marketplace is still diverse. By definition, the specific manner in which an international, regional, national, or market sector regulatory authority regulates depends on a variety of factors.[3]

Though there is admittedly no unified theory of financial services regulation, the following comprise some broad objectives for regulation:[4]

- Protecting investors to help build their confidence in the market
- Ensuring that the markets are fair, efficient, and transparent
- Reducing systemic risk
- Protecting financial services businesses from malpractice by some consumers (such as money laundering)
- Maintaining consumer confidence in the financial system.

Where the regulatory framework effectively controls market abuses, such as unlawful and unauthorized disclosures, insider dealing, and money laundering, prospects for building investor and consumer confidence in the market are high. Investors tend to target markets that protect them against such risks. And when financial intermediaries, market players, and institutional investors are well regulated, through means such as effective Chinese walls and clear codes of conduct, financial services businesses are likely to feel protected against fraudulent activity by consumers. Taken together with the efficient regulation of information disclosure, such efforts can lead to a more fair, efficient, and transparent market.

---

[3] *See* International Compliance Association, *International Diploma in Compliance— Manual* 1 (International Compliance Association 2003).

[4] *See id.* at 1–2. *See also* D. T. Llewellyn, *Institutional Structure of Financial Regulation and Supervision: The Basic Issues*, in *Aligning Financial Supervisory Structures with Country Needs* 36–37 (J. Carmichael, A. Fleming & D. Llewellyn eds., World Bank Institute 2004).

Systemic risk can be mitigated through efficient regulation of information and through the use of Chinese walls to fight contagion when certain parts of the market collapse. It is also important to ensure that legal rules are enforced so as to promote and maintain consumer confidence in the financial system. Rules without enforcement are like a tiger without teeth.

In general, the development of financial services regulation in many countries has followed a historic pattern. Among the factors that affect the pattern are public policy, the structure of the existing legal framework (including the national constitution, as in the case of Canada[5]), the impact of international best practices on various aspects of financial regulation, movements toward regional integration, a government's response to financial scandals (such as the collapse of Barings and BCCI in the United Kingdom, and the collapse of Enron in the United States), pressure from the international community, and market pressure in general.

One key objective of regulation is to redress the information imbalance that sometimes exists between consumers and financial services businesses in favor of consumers. This is usually done by imposing upon financial services businesses minimum standards of business conduct. Moreover, the fairness of the financial markets depends in part on the degree of consumer protection. Overall, regulation attempts to strike a balance, protecting the marketplace from itself without stifling legitimate risk-taking.[6] One method is to prevent business failures by imposing capital and internal control requirements. These requirements ensure that business entities have sufficient liquidity to meet their obligations, making them less vulnerable to hasty withdrawals by depositors and investors and to other market shocks.[7]

A number of countries have focused first on the regulation of banking (more specifically, deposit-taking activity) and investment (securities) businesses.[8] More recently, regulation has been introduced to control the conduct of trust and company services providers[9] and to curb financial crimes, such as money-laundering.[10] A legitimate question in all these cases is: What do we mean by "regulation"?

---

[5] On the Constitution-related argument regarding the structure of the regulatory framework for financial services supervision in Canada, *see generally* the following publications: *International Developments Part I, supra* n. 1; *International Developments Part II, supra* n. 1; and P. Kyle, *Making Regulatory Structures Effective: Establishing Legal Consistency for Integrated Regulation*, in J. Carmichael *et al.*, eds., *id.* at 211–14.

[6] International Compliance Association, *supra* n. 3, at 4.

[7] *See id.* at 4.

[8] *See id.* at 5.

[9] *See id.*

[10] *See generally* International Compliance Association, *International Diploma in Anti-Moneylaundering–Manual* (International Compliance Association 2003).

1.2   "Regulation" Defined

The term *regulation* refers to a set of binding rules issued by a private or public body.[11] Generally, these can be defined as those rules that are applied by all regulators in the fulfillment of their functions; in the financial services area, they include such prudential rules as those influencing the conditions of access to the market (intended to prevent the emergence of entities with doubtful reputation or without financial capacity necessary for the operations they intend to implement) and those aimed at controlling the risks associated with financial activities, corporate governance and internal control systems, conduct-of-business rules, and methods of supervision.[12] The body issuing these rules must be given the authority to do so.

Although some commentators, such as the International Compliance Association (ICA), have argued that the body issuing regulations should also have both the authority to supervise compliance with the rules and the power to issue sanctions against breach of the rules,[13] experience in many countries has shown that this is not always the case. There are situations where the power to issue regulations reposes in a different body from that handling sanctions for breach of regulations.

Also, the role of a regulator should not be confused with the role of a supervisor. Whereas a regulator is concerned mainly with preparing and issuing regulations and promoting a culture of compliance with these regulations, a supervisor, by contrast, may undertake on-site and off-site supervision of financial services businesses. In some jurisdictions, such as the UK, however, the powers to regulate and to supervise the activities of financial services businesses both reside in the same body.

The regulatory framework for financial services is often comprised of a combination of two or more of the following: (a) primary enabling legislation; (b) secondary legislation issued pursuant to the enabling statute; (c) principles, rules, and codes issued by regulators; and (d) guidance or policy directives issued by the regulatory authority. In some jurisdictions, primary legislation provides that "guidelines" should be treated as law.[14] In civil law countries, the civil code, which is the bloodline of private property rights in most civil law jurisdictions, can be equated to a constitution for the protection of private commercial and contractual rights of citizens. Though common law jurisdictions do not have the equivalent of a civil code, they can import and apply principles of the common law and doctrines of equity.

---

[11] International Compliance Association, *supra* n. 3, at 1.

[12] *See id.* at 46–48.

[13] *See id.* at 1.

[14] *See id.* at 22.

1.3   Designing a Framework for Financial Services Supervision

When a regulatory framework is designed, it is important that the drafters understand, first, the size and structure of a particular industry and, second, the role of a regulator in that country. In most jurisdictions, enormous power is bestowed upon regulators to authorize the commencement and cessation of businesses.[15] Regulators usually also have the power to make judgments about the conduct of individuals, which can have a profound impact on the ability of those individuals to work in the regulated sector.[16]

Invariably, the structure and objectives supporting the regulatory framework differ from one jurisdiction to another. In the U.S., for example, there are a multitude of agencies, at both the state and federal levels, that have separate yet sometimes duplicative regulatory authority over the financial services industry.[17] This high level of duplication is caused by a combination of functional and institutional regulation.[18] As one report for the United States shows:

> In the banking sector, for example, there are four regulators: (1) the Office of the Comptroller of the Currency; (2) the Federal Deposit Insurance Corporation; (3) the State Regulator; and (4) the Federal Reserve. In the securities arena, there is the Securities and Exchange Commission (SEC) and the Commodity Futures Trading Commission (CFTC). The securities business of investment banks is partly overseen by the SEC and partly by the Federal Reserve. There are different state regulators responsible for the conduct of the insurance business.[19]

Turning to other countries, the report notes that even in jurisdictions such as the UK or common law "offshore" jurisdictions where there is no hierarchy of different regulatory authorities, the environment is complex.[20] For instance,

---

[15] *See id.* at 39.

[16] *See id.*

[17] *See id. See also* S. A. Ramirez, *Depoliticizing Financial Regulation*, 41(2) Wm. & Mary L. Rev. (2000), http://classes.washburnlaw.edu/rami/publications/depoliticizing.htm (accessed June 28, 2004).

[18] On the functional and institutional models of financial regulation, *see generally* below, pp. 11–12.

[19] International Compliance Association, *supra* n. 3, at 16.

[20] *See id.* at 39–40.

regulators may fulfill the following functions:

- Lay down rules or principles that determine who can conduct a financial services business.
- Authorize financial services businesses to operate.
- Lay down rules for how those operating in the regulated industry must conduct their business (both prudential and conduct-of-business rules).
- Supervise compliance with the rules through desk-based supervision, onsite inspections, or a mixture of the two.
- Enforce the rules.
- Investigate suspected breaches of the rules, sometimes in conjunction with other law enforcement bodies.
- Cooperate and exchange information with other regulators.[21]

In some jurisdictions with less-developed regulatory regimes, regulators have been given a business development role.[22] However, this practice has been frowned upon by such groups as the International Monetary Fund (IMF) and the Financial Action Task Force (FATF) and those jurisdictions are moving away from the practice.[23]

There are a variety of models of financial services regulation throughout the world.[24] For example, in Hong Kong, while the Hong Kong Monetary Authority is in charge of the currency board and supervises banks, the Insurance Commissioner supervises insurance businesses,[25] the Securities and Futures Commission (SFC) supervises the securities and futures markets, and a Mandatory Provident Fund Authority oversees mandatory retirement funds.[26] By contrast, in most European Union (EU) countries, the central banks are responsible for banking supervision, although in Austria, Germany, Luxembourg, and Finland, this task is

---

[21] *See id.*

[22] *See id.*

[23] *See id.*

[24] *See*, for example, the conference papers collected in *Challenges for the Unified Financial Supervision in the New Millennium* (The World Bank & the Ministry of Finance of Estonia 2001).

[25] *See* International Monetary Fund, *Experimental IMF Report on Observance of Standards and Codes: People's Republic of China—Hong Kong Special Administrative Region*, http://www.imf.org/external/np/rosc/hkg/#V (accessed June 28, 2004). *See also* the website of the Hong Kong Monetary Authority, http://www.info.gov.hk/hkma/eng/hkma/index.htm (accessed June 28, 2004).

[26] International Compliance Association, *supra* n. 3, at 17.

TABLE 1.1

Financial Services Supervisory Models in the European Union

Country	Banking	Securities	Insurance
Belgium	BS	BS	I
Denmark	U	U	U
Germany	B	B, S	I
Greece	CB	S	I
Ireland	CB	CB	G
Italy	CB	CB, S	I
Luxembourg	BS	BS	I
France	B, CB	B, S	I
Spain	CB	S	I
Netherlands	CB	CB, S	I
Portugal	CB	CB, S	I
Austria	G	G	G
Finland	BS	BS	I
Sweden	U	U	U
United Kingdom	U	U	U

Explanatory notes: CB = Central bank; BS = Banking and securities supervisor;
B = Banking supervisor; S = Securities supervisor; I = Insurance supervisor;
G = Government department; and U = Single financial supervisor.

Source: International Compliance Association, *International Diploma in Compliance—Manual* (International Compliance Association, 2003).

assigned to a separate agency.[27] Table 1.1 illustrates the current structure of supervision in a number of EU countries.

Other common models of financial services regulation are regulation by objectives, functional regulation, institutional regulation (regulation by silos), and a single regulator.[28] In a system that subscribes to regulation by objectives, the regulatory model "seeks to achieve certain explicit objectives by giving responsibility for one or more of them to specific regulatory bodies that exist solely for that purpose."[29] Examples of this model are a central authority that is

---

[27] *See id.* at 18.

[28] *See id.* at 40. *See* D. T. Llewellyn, *supra* n. 4, at 40–50.

[29] International Compliance Association, *supra* n. 3, at 40.

empowered to conduct prudential regulation, a central authority responsible for supervising and passing regulations for the conduct of business, a central bank responsible for monetary policy, and a central authority responsible for regulating competition.[30]

In a system that pursues functional regulation,[31] there is a general view that it is more important to regulate the functions performed by financial services businesses than the types of businesses that undertake them.[32] This approach requires rules pertaining to function to be applied consistently to any business that discharges them, irrespective of the type of business.[33] Examples of functional activity that can be regulated across all sectors include client assets and all conduct-of-business issues. Australia, for instance, has a "twin peaks" regulatory model that adopts a functional regulation approach:[34]

(1) The Australian Securities and Investment Commission (ASIC) looks after market regulation and consumer protection (referred to as "market conduct regulation"). ASIC is also responsible for financial sector consumer protection.[35]

(2) The Australian Prudential Regulatory Authority (APRA) is responsible for prudential regulation.

Meanwhile, the Reserve Bank of Australia looks after monetary policy and systemic stability.

Clearly, there is no simple panacea for a government or country in its choice of a regulatory model. Various country-specific factors, including the policy objectives underpinning the choice of a regulatory model, the development and sophistication of the financial sector, and groups of companies that are closely interconnected, thus posing a greater threat of systemic risk and contagion, can influence the choice of a particular regulatory model.

In general, the idea of *institutional* regulation, unlike that of *functional* regulation, relates to the regulation of each single category of financial services

---

[30] *See id.* at 40–41.

[31] Functional regulation is sometimes referred to as "regulation by activity."

[32] International Compliance Association, *supra* n. 3, at 41.

[33] *See id.* at 41.

[34] *See id.*

[35] *See id.* at 41 and 17. *See also* The Hon. Peter Costello, MP, Treasurer of the Commonwealth of Australia, Treasurer Address to CCH Forum, *Australia's Financial Services Reform Agenda* (Sydney, July 17, 2003), http://www.treasurer.gov.au/tsr/content/speeches/2003/009.asp (accessed June 28, 2004).

business by a different authority, agency, or agency division.[36] This model is sometimes referred to as "regulation by silos" or "the by-markets regulatory model." According to one commentator, the distinction between functional and institutional regulation is one of the jurisprudential bases for the choice of regulation; the concept of a unified regulator is almost the antithesis of institutional regulation.[37]

While this view may hold water, it is not immediately clear that the choice of functional over institutional regulation, or vice versa, reflects the *raison d'être*— the philosophical foundation—for why a country should or should not introduce unified financial services supervision. From much of the data gathered in a seminal study on unified financial services supervision, covering countries as varied as Iceland, Hungary, Canada, Denmark, Norway, Sweden, Poland, Bulgaria, and the United Kingdom, it was observed that, in many cases, models of unified financial services supervision started out along the lines of institutional before graduating into functional regulation.[38] In short, this is not a simple choice between institutional regulation and functional regulation. Nor are the two entirely opposed. They can complement one another, providing a country with mixed and rational attributes of both institutional and functional regulation, or one system can run as a precursor to the other.

A major difference between functional and institutional regulation is that the former emphasizes the setting up of departments in a supervisory agency that deal with such nonsectoral functions as licensing, legal, accounting, enforcement, and information technology, irrespective of the type of business activity being regulated. By contrast, a silo or institutional regulatory model encourages organization into departments that deal separately with all aspects of specific types of business activities. For example, the silo model could separately address banking, insurance, pension funds, and trading in securities, while the functional model would concern itself mainly with finding out whether the issue to be dealt with is one of licensing or any other regulatory norm, irrespective of the type of business activity.

A single regulator, commonly referred to as a "unified" regulator,[39] is another model of financial services regulation. There is, again, no single right way of

---

[36] International Compliance Association, *supra* n. 3, at 41.

[37] E-mail from Nagavalli Annamalai, Lead Counsel, Private Sector, Finance and Infrastructure Development Group (LEGPS), The World Bank, to the author (March 31, 2005) (copy on file with the author).

[38] *See generally*, *International Developments Parts I* and *II*, *supra* n. 1; K. K. Mwenda, *supra* n. 1.

[39] *See id.*

structuring a unified regulator. Some have jurisdiction, as a single central authority, to regulate different institutions and functions and monitor fulfillment of all regulatory objectives.[40] Some deal solely with the securities and insurance industries, or solely with pension funds and insurance companies. In the UK, for example, the Financial Services Authority (FSA) has taken over the supervisory and regulatory roles previously carried out by some self-regulatory organizations (SROs) and statutory boards, such as the Securities and Investment Board, the Investment Management Regulatory Authority, the Securities and Futures Authority, the Personal Investment Authority, the Friendly Societies Commission, the Registry of Friendly Societies, the Insurance Directorate of the Department of Trade and Industry, the Building Societies Commission, Lloyds of London, the UK Listing Authority, and the Supervision and Surveillance Department of the Bank of England.[41] Indeed, the supervisory and regulatory mandate of FSA covers a whole range of banking, insurance, securities, and mutual fund activities.[42] Further, the FSA is responsible for promoting and protecting consumer interests,[43] and it cooperates closely and exchanges information with the Bank of England and the Treasury: A memorandum of understanding, published in 1997, provides a framework for coordination of FSA, Bank of England, and Treasury functions. Similar memoranda of understanding have been executed in other countries, such as Hungary and Zambia.[44]

In the final analysis, for any country the choice of regulatory model depends on a variety of factors, some of which, as we saw earlier, are country-specific. Among these factors may be the historical development of the financial services industry as well as such factors already alluded to as public policy priorities and government efforts to move toward regional integration. With this in mind, we now examine the concepts of a principles-based system of regulation and of rules-based regulation.

---

[40] *See* International Compliance Association, *supra* n. 3, at 41.

[41] *See id.* at 17.

[42] *See id.*

[43] *See id.*

[44] *See* K. K. Mwenda, *Unified Financial Services Regulation: The Unfolding Debate*, 1(2) CHIMERA J. 25–30 (2003), http://www.usaafrica.org/Chimera-Summer03.html (accessed January 2, 2005); and K. K. Mwenda & A Fleming, *Developments in Unified Financial Services Supervision: An International and Comparative Perspective*, in *Challenges for the Unified Financial Services Supervision in the New Millennium*, *supra* n. 24 at 172–77.

1.3.1   Principles-based or Rules-based Regulation?

The design of a regulatory framework for financial services can be motivated by the need to introduce either principles- or rules-based regulation; the difference can be summarized as follows:

> A principles-based system, which is common to most offshore financial centres, is one in which regulators simply issue a set of principles with which regulated businesses must comply. They are generally supplemented by broad codes. In a rules-based system (for example, the UK), regulatory bodies also impose principles of regulation and supplement them with detailed "rules" with which regulated businesses must abide in the fulfilment of those principles.[45]

In both cases, financial and human capital resources should be made available to support the design and implementation of an efficient regulatory framework. Also, there is need to galvanize the necessary political will among different stakeholders.

Further, where a regulator, unified or not, is housed (such as in the central bank or elsewhere) is another issue the country must decide, weighing its choice against the resources it has and against the policy objectives underpinning the introduction of the new regulatory framework. Some regulatory bodies have started off by piggybacking on the central bank or the Ministry of Finance for office accommodation, or began as a department of the central bank or the Ministry. Others have from the very beginning been organized and housed separately. Among the factors affecting the decision may be organizational politics, limited financial resources, insufficient numbers of appropriately qualified personnel, difficulties in identifying or financing the acquisition of offices to accommodate the regulator, and the stakeholder interests of an institution such as the central bank in the new regulatory body.

1.4   General Statutory Powers of a Regulatory Body

Most effective regulatory bodies, whatever the jurisdiction in which they operate, have clear responsibilities and objectives, adequate powers, adequate resources, transparency, and accountability.[46] Generally, the responsibilities and objectives of such a body depend in part on the regulatory model in place and the role the regulator has been established to fulfill.[47] It has been argued, for example, that a

---

[45] *See* International Compliance Association, *supra* n. 3, at 41.

[46] *See id.* at 49.

[47] *See id.*

regulator must have sufficient legal powers to make regulation effective, such as the power to

- authorize businesses to conduct regulated activities;
- supervise regulated businesses;
- inspect, investigate, and enforce compliance with legal and regulatory requirements, either through imposition of license requirements or withdrawal of authorization; and
- share information with other regulators.

To facilitate application of these powers, the law should also provide the regulator with protection against any liability that may arise from the proper discharge of its powers. In many countries, primary legislation protects regulators from liability arising out of the exercise of any of their powers unless the regulators exercise those powers in bad faith.[48] The protection of regulators is important; it gives them an incentive to perform diligently, competently, independently, and professionally, without fear that they will be sued by an aggrieved party, even if they had acted in good faith, for torts such as negligence or trespass.

A common criticism by international evaluators is that many regulators lack the resources they need to fulfill their functions.[49] Lack of resources can compromise a regulator's independence if the regulator is heavily reliant on the state to fund its operations. For instance, in many countries, bank supervisors receive better remuneration and perquisites than, say, insurance supervisors, securities regulators, or pension fund supervisors. Such a disparity can create tensions when the different supervisors are all brought under one roof. Bank supervisors would want to maintain their compensation, while their counterparts in the non-banking financial sectors would want to be raised to the bank supervisors' financial level. Questions may well surface as to whether the salaries of all supervisors should be harmonized across the unified agency based on qualifications, work experience, or the industry supervised. If this matter is not handled properly, the unified agency risks losing well-qualified staff to the private sector. The private sector is likely to pay these individuals better than the regulator, although the regulator may have invested heavily in training these individuals.

Another area where some regulators face resource constraints relates to an inability to hire well-qualified people to perform certain supervisory tasks. The lack of appropriately qualified human capital is a notable constraint on regulatory agencies, especially in developing countries and emerging economies. Equally

---

[48] *See id.* at 50.

[49] *See id.*

important as the human resource constraint is the lack of suitable infrastructure and technology to process information in a timely and reliable manner. Again, many regulatory agencies in developing countries and emerging economies are confronted by this problem.

In general, the issue of how independent a regulator should be has generated considerable debate on the disadvantages and advantages of the very concept of an independent regulator. A common view, however, is that a regulator should be operationally independent and accountable for the use of its powers.[50] The following indicators are characteristic of a regulator with accountability: operations that are independent of political and commercial interests and that are transparent; the right of appeal of the regulator's decisions; and access to judicial review of the regulator's decisions.[51] Regulatory bodies often seek to achieve transparency and accountability by imposing both internal and external safeguards.[52]

1.4.1 Authorization to Conduct a Financial Services Business

Generally, the power to authorize an individual or business entity to conduct a financial services business is vested in the regulator,[53] and only when authorization is granted, usually in the form of an operating license, may an organization proceed to undertake the activity it is authorized to conduct. In many jurisdictions, undertaking regulated business activity without the necessary authorization is a criminal offense.[54] In deciding whether to authorize a financial services business, regulators tend to assess the following aspects of a business:

- Fitness of the organizers (honesty, integrity, reputation, competence, ability and organization, and financial position)
- Scope of the business and business profile and plan (strategy and management responsibilities)
- Compliance procedures and activities (staff training, operating procedures, in-house rules, monitoring, handling of customer complaints, and notification requirements)

---

[50] *See id.*

[51] *See id.*

[52] *See id.*

[53] *See id.* at 42.

[54] *See* K. K. Mwenda, *Legal Aspects of Corporate Finance: The Case for an Emerging Stock Market,* unpublished Ph.D. thesis 270–82 (University of Warwick 1998); and K. K. Mwenda, *Zambia's Stock Exchange and Privatisation Programme: Corporate Finance Law in Emerging Markets* 192–218 (Edwin Mellen Press 2001).

- Management (qualifications and experience, independence of risk and control management, conflicts of interest, reporting and management information)
- Resources (financial, human, and information technology resources; training; compliance; front and back office organization).[55]

Where the proposed owner or parent organization of a financial services business is a foreign financial institution, it is usually prudent, as a prerequisite to authorization, to consult with the agency responsible for supervision of the entity in its home country. The host regulator should seek confirmation from the home regulator that the branch or subsidiary is subject to consolidated supervision and a decision should be made about who is the lead regulator for the organization. In many jurisdictions, regulators have signed memoranda of understanding both with other regulators within their jurisdictions and with regulators in foreign jurisdictions. These memoranda are useful in facilitating the sharing of information between regulators as they investigate financial services businesses engaged in crossborder and multisector transactions. Common terms in such memoranda are clauses dealing with the scope of assistance, the necessary forms of request for assistance, permissible uses of information, and confidentiality.[56]

1.4.2   Supervision of Financial Services Businesses

Some regulators have statutory powers only to issue regulations and to ensure, through oversight, that they are complied with. Other supervisory powers are left to other bodies. In this section, however, we proceed on the assumption that the regulator has powers to both issue regulations and supervise financial services businesses.

In general, the elements of the process of regulation are as follows:

(a) Defining the objectives;
(b) Obtaining information from regulated businesses;
(c) Assessing the risk that regulated businesses pose; and
(d) Taking action in response to the risk assessment.[57]

Given that no business is without risk, many regulators adopt a risk-based approach to supervision,[58] ensuring that the various types of risk associated with

---

[55] *See* International Compliance Association, *supra* n. 3, at 42–43.

[56] *See id.* at 52.

[57] *See id.* at 43.

[58] *See id.*

a particular financial services industry or business are identified, quantified, managed, and monitored properly.

1.4.3 Enforcement of Regulations

Many countries today consider enforcement of the rules for the financial services industry to be part of the function of a regulator. It has been argued, for example, that:

> Enforcement is a necessary product of the process of authorisation and supervision, in the sense that a regulator must enforce compliance with rules. A broad range of enforcement action exists, not all of which necessarily results in the imposition of regulatory penalties upon a business. It is, for example, perfectly normal for a regulator to commence enforcement action by conducting an investigation which may lead to vindication of a business and its employees. Thus enforcement is as much about investigating, gathering and sharing information as it is about imposing penalties.[59]

Requiring a regulator to enforce rules entails giving the regulator responsibility for carrying out inspections, investigations, and surveillance, and imposing remedial action and penalties.[60] In jurisdictions where this occurs, regulators normally have powers to request information, impose sanctions, seek orders from courts or other tribunals, refer matters for criminal prosecution, and suspend business operations or trading.[61] International standard-setting bodies have been promoting the importance of domestic regulators having adequate enforcement powers.[62]

1.5 Conclusion

This chapter has examined critical issues relating to establishment of a sound regulatory and institutional framework for the supervision of financial services. The chapter examined, *inter alia*, the objectives of financial services regulation, different models of financial services regulation, and the different roles of financial services regulators, and identified essential elements of a sound framework for the supervision of financial services. It was also pointed out that there is no unified theory of financial services regulation. The chapter fleshed out some of

---

[59] *See id.* at 45.

[60] *See id.*

[61] *See id.*

[62] *See id.*

the common conceptual and practical issues that arise in setting up a sound regulatory and institutional framework for financial services supervision, emphasizing the diversity of the financial services industry. It was concluded that the structure of the regulatory and institutional framework in every country will depend in part on the objectives of regulation and the size of the financial sector, and that the type of risk control systems in place and their effectiveness can affect the regulatory and institutional structure.

CHAPTER **2**

Promoting the Independence of a Financial Services Regulator

2.1 Introduction

The preceding chapter examined the historical development of unified financial services supervision. While Chapter 3 considers the concept of a unified financial services regulator by looking at approaches taken in a variety of countries, this chapter examines the idea of promoting the independence of a financial services regulator as a corollary to designing an efficient and effective national framework for financial services supervision. It asks such questions as: Should law reform professionals, policy makers, and institutions concerned with creating legal frameworks for financial services supervision bother about imbuing in the law the concept of an independent regulator? What are the key features or themes to consider when promoting the independence of a financial services regulator?

This chapter examines, *inter alia*, the conceptual, theoretical, and practical advantages of a country having an independent regulator rather than a regulator whose independence is compromised by such factors as political interference from the government. It discusses economic, jurisprudential, and policy considerations underpinning a sound regulatory and institutional framework for financial services supervision. It is argued that, although independence provides incentives for regulators to improve the quality of their supervision, it may not necessarily prevent the occurrence of a financial crisis. The cardinal point, it avers, is that both political independence and independence from the industry regulated are as important as ensuring that the independent regulator is accountable.

2.2 Independence and the Financial Services Regulator

The concept of independent regulation has come to be associated more with the service sector than with the goods sector.[63] Examining the idea of central bank independence, Nobel Laureate Joseph Stiglitz, former Chief Economist of the

---

[63] *See* P. S. Mehta, *Why a Steel Regulator Makes Little Sense*, Business Line (December 17, 2004), http://cuts-international.org/articles2004.htm (accessed January 3, 2005).

World Bank, puts it succinctly:

> An independent central bank focused exclusively on price stability has become a central part of the mantra of "economic reform." Like so many other policy maxims, it has been repeated often enough that it has come to be believed. But bold assertions, even from central bankers, are no substitute for research and analysis.
>
> Research suggests that if central banks focus on inflation, they do a better job at controlling inflation. But controlling inflation is not an end in itself: it is merely a means of achieving faster, more stable growth, with lower unemployment.
>
> These are the *real* variables that matter, and there is little evidence that independent central banks focusing exclusively on price stability do better in these crucial respects. . . .
>
> The economic analysis of Clinton's Council of Economic Advisers turned out to be right; the models of the IMF (and the Fed) were wrong.[64]

While the term "independence," in its ordinary meaning, could entail the idea of not being influenced or controlled by others, the independence of any regulatory agency can be viewed from four related angles: regulatory, supervisory, institutional, and budgetary.[65] *Regulatory independence* in the financial sector means that regulators have wide autonomy in setting, at a minimum, prudential regulations that follow from the special nature of financial intermediation.[66] These regulations concern practices that financial institutions must adopt to maintain their safety and stability, including minimum capital adequacy ratios, exposure limits, and loan provisioning.[67] It has been argued that regulators who are able to set these rules independently are more likely to be motivated to enforce them.[68] But is the fact that the regulators and supervising financial services business are independent an end in itself, or should these regulators also be committed to transparency and accountability?

We will examine these issues in greater detail in the next section. Here, suffice it to say that, while the independence of a regulator can at times be achieved by

---

[64] J. Stiglitz, *Big Lies About Central Banking*, Project Syndicate, http://www.project-syndicate.org/commentaries/commentary_text.php4?id=1232&m&setcookie=1 (accessed January 3, 2005).

[65] M. Quintyn & M. W. Taylor, *Should Financial Sector Regulators Be Independent?* 34 Economic Issues 6 (IMF 2004).

[66] *See id.* at 6–7.

[67] *See id.* at 7.

[68] *See id.*

giving the regulator legal and operational autonomy, or financial autonomy, or by establishing procedures for the independent appointment and dismissal of regulators, or even through the composition of the regulatory agency itself, confidence in the quality of oversight can be compromised where the regulator's independence is challenged or threatened. Close relationships between regulators and the institutions and individuals they regulate are often a cause of concern.

Although *supervisory independence* is crucial to the financial sector, it may prove difficult to establish and guarantee, since supervisors often work closely with financial institutions not only in inspecting and monitoring them but also in enforcing sanctions and even revoking licenses. Further, because much supervisory activity takes place outside direct public view, interference, either by politicians or by industry, can be subtle, taking many forms.[69] Thus,

> Steps to protect supervisors' integrity include offering legal protection (for example, repealing laws that, in some countries, allow supervisors to be sued personally for their work) and providing financial incentives that allow supervisory agencies to attract and keep competent staff and discourage bribery. Crafting a rules-based system of sanctions and interventions also lessens the scope for supervisory discretion—and thus for political or industry interference. To protect supervisors from political or industry intimidation during a lengthy court process, banking law should also limit the time allowed for appeals by institutions facing sanctions. Independent supervisors, not a government agency or minister, should be given sole authority to grant and withdraw licenses because they best understand the financial sector's proper composition—and because the threat to revoke a license is a powerful supervisory tool.[70]

Closely related to the idea of the supervisory independence of a regulator is that of *institutional independence* and the agency's status outside the executive and legislative branches of government.[71] There are several ways in which the institutional and supervisory independence of a regulator can be assessed. For example, where there is a high turnover of senior executives of a regulatory agency, where there appears to be poor exercise of discretionary powers, where there is evidence of abuse of regulatory forbearance, where a regulator seems increasingly to be acting under external pressures and limitations, or where a regulator, in spite of being well endowed with resources, is failing to exercise its powers effectively, the independence of that regulator is questionable. Also, a regulator that cannot set licensing fees for market participants or execute any of its enforcement functions

---

[69] *See id.*

[70] *See id.*

[71] *See id.* at 8.

has insufficient independence. Here, it is important to stress that the independence gives the regulator incentives to adopt best practices of corporate governance and accountability. Where corporate governance and accountability appear to be poor that raises concerns about the independence of the regulator.

Taking the banking sector as an example, a central bank that is too susceptible to political direction or pressure can end up exacerbating economic cycles ("boom and bust"), because politicians are likely to be tempted to boost the economy in advance of an election, to the detriment of the long-term health of the economy. Ideally, an independent central bank can run a more credible monetary policy, making market expectations more responsive to signals from the central bank. The issue of central bank independence has been examined in greater detail elsewhere.[72] Here, the salient features of the discussion will be highlighted.

2.3   The Example of Central Bank Independence

While the worldwide trend toward central bank independence[73] has its roots in a number of factors, the most fundamental was a challenge to economic orthodoxy that occurred in the 1970s.[74] Taylor argues that the original nationalization of the Bank of England had taken place within a policy context that seemed to accept the need for governments deliberately to stimulate demand in the economy to ensure constant high levels of output and employment.[75]

This policy was largely inspired by the economic theories of John Maynard Keynes, and hence became known as the Keynesian demand manage-

---

[72] K. K. Mwenda, *Banking Supervision and Systemic Bank Restructuring: An International and Comparative Legal Perspective* 103–107 (Cavendish Publishing 2000).

[73] For further readings on this topic, *see generally* A. Alesina & R. Gatti, *Independent Central Banks: Low Inflation at No Costs*, 85 Am. Econ. Rev., Papers and Proceedings 196–200 (1995); C. Bean, *The New UK Monetary Arrangement: A View from the Literature*, 108 Econ. J. 1795–1809 (1998); R. M. W. J. Beetsma & A. L. Bovenberg, *Central Bank Independence and Public Debt Policy*, 12 J. Econ. Dynamics & Control 873–894 (1997); A. P. Blake & M. Weale, *Costs of Separating Budgetary Policy from Control of Inflation: A Neglected Aspect of Central Bank Independence*, 50 Oxford Econ. Papers 449–467 (1998); C. B. Briault, A. G. Haldane & M. A. King, *Independence and Accountability*, 49 Bank of England Working Paper (1996); G. Debelle, *Central Bank Independence: A Free Lunch?* IMF Working Paper, No. 96/1 (1996); G. Debelle & S. Fischer, *How Independent Should a Central Bank Be?* in *Goals, Guidelines, and Constraints Facing Monetary Policy Makers*, Federal Reserve Bank of Boston Conference Series, No. 38 (J. C. Fuhrer ed., 1994); A. Posen, *Central Bank Independence and Disinflationary Credibility: A Missing Link*, 50 Oxford Econ. Papers 335–59 (1998); and L. E. O. Svensson, *Inflation Targeting: Implementing and Monitoring Inflation Targets*, 41 Eur. Econ. Rev. 1111–46 (1997).

[74] M. Taylor, *Central Bank Independence: The Policy Background*, in M. Blair, R. Cranston, C. Ryan & M. Taylor, *Blackstone's Guide to the Bank of England Act 1998* 10 (Blackstone Press Limited 1998).

[75] *See id.* at 11.

ment. . . . In the first few decades of the post-war era governments sought to use their power to tax, borrow and spend ("fiscal policy") to ensure that unemployment stayed low. Inflation was not seen as a serious threat, and a modest amount could be accepted as the price of protecting jobs. Thus monetary policy was regarded as a subsidiary to fiscal policy as the main lever for influencing the level of economic activity, and interest rates were deliberately kept down to stimulate investment. In this environment it was natural to expect the central bank to play a subordinate role to government, and to follow policies which supported the broad policy objective of ensuring against the return to the mass unemployment of the 1930s.

This orthodoxy began to break down in the early 1970s. Governments throughout the developed world were then faced by both rising unemployment and rising inflation, something the Keynesian model of the economy failed to predict. The failure of demand-management policies permitted the emergence of a new economic orthodoxy which stressed the importance of controlling inflation as the key to ensuring successful long-term economic performance.[76]

Some decades later, following a shift in October 1992 to inflation targeting by the British government that was relatively successful for four and a half years, the government granted operational independence to the Bank of England.[77] Under the new arrangement, the inflation target is set by the Chancellor of the Exchequer in the annual budget; then the Monetary Policy Committee (MPC)—established following the decision to grant the bank independence and consisting of Bank of England staff members and outsiders—sets interest rates to achieve the inflation target.[78] While the basic idea is not entirely new, inflation targeting is a rather significant step toward establishing a workable and well-defined framework for monetary policy.

A fundamental implication of central bank independence is the separation of monetary and fiscal policies, which has a virtually unavoidable impact on the policy mix.[79] It is often argued that monetary policy is constrained by excessive gradualism, in the sense that decision making seeks to smooth interest rates relative to some optimal rule.[80] The IMF notes that the granting of operational independence to the Bank of England has made decision making more transparent, focused, and analytical.[81] The significance of the fact that inflation targeting uses

---

[76] *See id.* at 10–11.

[77] H. Samiei, J. K. Martijn, Z. Kontolemis & L. Bartolini, *International Monetary Fund: United Kingdom. Selected Issues* 4 (IMF 1999).

[78] *See id.* at 4.

[79] *See id.* at 17.

[80] *See id.* at 4.

[81] *See id.*

expected rather than actual inflation as an operational target (or as intermediate target) is seen in the following:

> [The use of expected inflation] implies that factors, such as the output gap and fiscal policy, that play a role in the determination of future inflation should in principle enter the decision-making process, as well as the expectations of their path and future interest rate decisions. For example, tight product and labor markets would be expected to raise inflation and, within the inflation targeting framework, generate a monetary policy response even before actual inflation rose. Given the estimated lags between monetary policy and inflation, such forward-looking behavior is necessary to achieve the target.[82]

Despite all the improvements to monetary policy in the UK, and also given the apparent success of targeting in controlling inflation, the new regime arguably did not sufficiently protect against inflationary bias.[83] The "government remained in control of the policy process, and no institutional safeguards existed against the use of unsustainable politically motivated monetary policy decisions."[84] It was not until May 1997 that the UK government took measures to remedy this deficiency by giving operational independence to the Bank of England.

The advantages of central bank independence vary from context to context. Some consider that central bank independence can increase the credibility of monetary policy by convincing private agents that the monetary authority has little incentive to create surprise inflation.[85] Further, the mere granting of central bank independence "would likely suffice to remove the distortion"[86] in political business cycles such as where the government in power, seeking to win an election, directs the central bank to finance part of the election campaign. On the other hand, there is a likelihood of encountering some shortcomings if central bank independence is introduced without due consideration of its objective function. The objective function is often driven by economic policies of a government. For example, where there is permanent inflation bias associated with time-inconsistent policies, given that surprise inflation would be the equilibrium outcome, the mere introduction of central bank independence, without reference to its objective function, would neither be a sufficient step nor a credible commitment to price stability.[87] However, where a policy such as inflation targeting

---

[82] *See id.* at 7.

[83] *See id.*

[84] *See id.*

[85] *See id.* at 10.

[86] *See id.*

[87] *See id.*

is combined with the operational independence of the central bank, as in the United Kingdom now, there is a suitable framework for a focused and credible monetary policy that is effective in reducing the inflationary bias in policy making.[88]

2.4   Independent but Accountable

In many countries, policy makers and policy analysts are increasingly recognizing the need to shield financial sector regulators from political pressure.[89] Measures to do so help to improve the quality of regulation, with the ultimate goal of preventing financial crises.[90] It is not enough that the regulator that supervises financial services is independent. To be efficient and effective, the independent regulator must also be transparent and accountable.[91] For this reason, *institutional independence* has three critical elements:

1. Senior personnel should enjoy security of tenure (clear rules, ideally involving two government bodies that govern their appointment and, especially, dismissal, or a single body that is bound by legislation governing the grounds for the appointment and dismissal of senior personnel, with a possibility provided to aggrieved parties to appeal against the dismissal decisions).
2. The agency's governance structure should incorporate multimember commissions composed of experts.
3. Decision making should be transparent to a degree consistent with commercial confidentiality, enabling both the public and the industry to scrutinize regulatory decisions.[92]

Budgetary independence, on the other hand, is said to depend primarily on the role of the executive or the legislative branch that determines the agency's budget and how it is used.[93] This means that supervisors should not be subjected to

---

[88] *See id.* at 21.

[89] *See* K. K. Mwenda, *supra* n. 72, at 104–107.

[90] M. Quintyn & M. W. Taylor, *supra* n. 65, at 1.

[91] For similar views, but focusing on prospects for setting up a unified financial services regulator in the Bahamas, *see* Nassau Guardian, *The Rationale for a Single National Financial Services Regulator: Is The Bahamas Ready for a Super Regulator?* http://www.thenassauguardian.com/business/295537629381368.php# (March 9, 2004, accessed January 2, 2005).

[92] M. Quintyn & M. W. Taylor, *supra* n. 65, at 8.

[93] *See id.* at 8.

political pressure through the budget. Also, if funding of the regulatory agency must come from the government budget, then the supervisory budget should be proposed and justified by the agency itself, following objective criteria related to what is happening in the market.[94]

Some supervisory agencies are funded through industry fees. While it does minimize political interference, this practice, it must be emphasized, risks increasing dependence on—and interference from—the industry.[95] Therefore, if industry fees are to be used to fund regulation, they should be determined jointly by the regulatory agency and the government.[96] Also, given that fee-based funding may leave the agency strapped for funds during a crisis, which is precisely when businesses in the industry are most likely to have difficulty paying the fee, regulatory agencies should be allowed to build up reserve funds as insurance.[97]

In many countries, politicians define regulatory and supervisory goals in the same way that they set a country's targets for monetary policy, but it is the regulators, like the central bank as is customary in the case of monetary policy, that determine how to achieve these goals. Thus, where regulators fail, they should be held accountable, since they determine how to achieve regulatory goals.[98] But does the independence of the regulator necessarily guarantee the quality of regulation? And can the fact that a financial services regulator is seen as independent prevent a financial crisis?

In assessing the efficacy of the legal, regulatory, and institutional frameworks for financial services supervision, among issues to consider that are fundamental to an efficient and effective framework is the question of how independent financial services regulators are, or should be. Although independence may provide an incentive for improving the quality of regulation, it may not necessarily prevent a financial crisis. (The other structural, macro-, and microeconomic conditions that need to be taken into account are beyond the scope of this chapter.)

Before examining some of the arguments for and against the idea of an independent financial sector regulator, let us identify some of the questions to be answered in assessing the efficacy of legal, regulatory, and institutional

---

[94] *See id.*

[95] *See id.*

[96] *See id.*

[97] *See id.*

[98] *See* C. Proctor, *Regulatory Immunity and Legal Risk*, 7(3) Financial Regulator 27 (2002). http://www.centralbanking.co.uk/publications/journals/pdf/FR_7_3_Proctor.pdf (accessed January 2, 2005).

frameworks for financial services supervision. They are closely related to the idea of how independent financial services regulators are or should be.

- Is the governance structure of the financial services regulator based on sound principles of corporate governance?[99]
- Within the legal and regulatory framework, is there a balance between the concept of an independent regulator and that of accountability of the regulator?
- Who has powers to appoint and dismiss the Chief Executive Officer (CEO) of the financial services regulator?
- What are the minimum qualifications for appointment as CEO of a financial services regulator?
- Is the CEO appointed by the Minister or the Head of State?
- Alternatively, is the CEO appointed by Parliament? Does Parliament have the legal authority to remove the CEO from office?
- Are the grounds on which the CEO can be fired spelled out clearly in the law?
- Does the Minister or the Head of State have wide discretionary powers to hire and fire the CEO?
- Are decisions of the regulatory agency arrived at in a transparent manner, though with due deference to the need for client confidentiality?
- Who determines the salaries of the CEO and the directors of the regulator?
- Does the Ministry of Finance or any other Government Ministry determine the salaries and appoint the directors?
- Who determines and funds the operational and administrative budget of the regulator?
- Are financial services regulators civil servants and who determines their conditions of service?
- Are these regulators immune from lawsuits for omissions or acts done in good faith in the course of business?
- When, and under what circumstances, can financial services regulators be held liable for omissions or acts done in the course of business?
- Does the Minister have powers to intervene in the functions of the regulator?
- Does the legal framework address adequately the issue of disclosure of information, and are there continuing disclosure obligations?
- To what extent does the legal framework deal with matters such as unauthorized securities advertisements, misleading statements and misrepresentations, creation of a false market in securities, market abuse, and insider dealing?

---

[99] *See* D. T. Llewellyn, *supra* n. 4, at 30.

- What are the conditions for authorizing and licensing financial intermediaries? On what grounds can licenses be suspended or withdrawn?
- Does the legal framework provide for a compensation fund to protect investors, or for an ombudsman or a code of conduct to regulate financial intermediaries?
- Does the regulatory and institutional framework meet international standards and best practices, such as the Basel Core Principles for Effective Banking Supervision or the Basel Accord II?[100]
- What are the legal requirements for listing securities, licensing banks, licensing securities firms, and licensing insurance and pension fund companies?
- What are the grounds upon which securities can be suspended from listing or de-listed?
- What are the grounds for de-licensing or deregistration of banks, securities firms, insurance companies, and pension fund companies?
- Does the legal framework give regulators sweeping powers of regulatory forbearance? Are such powers used arbitrarily and for political reasons?

The question whether an independent regulator can promote the quality of regulation and supervision cannot be answered fully without examining a number of the issues just raised. Equally important are other critical issues, such as:

- Is the country a civil law or a common law jurisdiction and what are the implications of this?
- If a civil law system, does its Civil Code contain regulatory norms or rules that affect the legal, regulatory, and institutional framework for financial services supervision?
- If a common law system, are there doctrines of equity that can be imported into the legal and regulatory frameworks, and have these doctrines and the attendant fiduciary duties of financial intermediaries been codified?
- Should a financial services regulator cite central bank independence as a basis of its own independence? Would such an approach compromise the independence of the financial services regulator where the regulator is housed within the central bank and is likely to be drawing on its resources?
- What measures should be taken to ensure that a financial services regulator remains independent of the central bank?

A typical example of problems that can arise when a financial services regulator is too closely connected to the central bank can be seen in the case of

---

[100] *See generally*, http://www.bis.org/.

Ireland. Debating the Central Bank and Financial Services Authority of Ireland Bill 2002 before the Parliament of Ireland, a Mr. Naughten observed:

> Section 27 of this Bill . . . provides that the Governor of the Central Bank may issue guidelines to the regulatory authority. This calls into question the independence of the regulator, as it may be the case that he or she will be subservient to the bank itself. Consequently, the director of consumer affairs within the regulatory authority, who is subservient to the chief executive of the regulatory authority, is also subservient to the chief executive of the bank. There seems to be a conflict in the fact that an authority that was originally intended to stand alone and have independent powers to ensure regulation within the industry will now have to report continually to the Central Bank.

> The staff of the new authority will be recruited from within the Central Bank and the Departments of Enterprise, Trade and Employment and Finance. The new agency's officials will naturally have a certain bias as a result of their previous experiences. The chief executive of the new body does not have the independence to appoint his or her own officials, as they will have to come from the Central Bank or the Departments. Such provisions cast doubt on the ability of the new authority to maintain the independence it will require. The Minister for Enterprise, Trade and Employment indicated confidence that such independence can be achieved in her response to the publication of this Bill, but many people who have commented on the Bill since its publication are not convinced.[101]

Other issues that should be considered when examining the concept of an independent financial services regulator include:

- What impact would rampant corruption in either the financial services industry and the civil service have on the efficacy of the legal, regulatory, and institutional framework for financial services supervision?
- If a financial services regulator is part of the civil service, and is housed in the Ministry of Finance, how independent could the regulator be and to what extent can the regulator be shielded from corrupt practices?

A notoriously troubling experience for several countries is political interference in the decision-making process of financial services regulators. Quintyn and Taylor argue that in nearly every major financial crisis of the past decade—from East Asia to Russia, Turkey, and Latin America—political interference in financial

---

[101] Tithe an Oireachitais, Parliament of Ireland, *Central Bank and Financial Services Authority of Ireland Bill*, 2002: Second Stage (Resumed), Daily Debates, http://www.irlgov.ie/debates-02/19Jun/Sect2.htm (accessed January 2, 2005).

sector regulation made a bad situation worse.[102] The authors observe that political pressures not only weakened financial regulation generally but they also hindered those who enforce the regulations from taking action against banks that ran into trouble.[103] In so doing, Quintyn and Taylor assert,[104] political pressures crippled the financial sector in the run-up to the crisis, delayed recognition of the severity of the crisis, slowed needed intervention, and raised the cost of the crisis to taxpayers. In countries where financial services regulators lacked independence, that tended to worsen the crisis.[105]

> In many of the world's recent financial crises, policy makers in the countries affected have sought to intervene in the work of regulators—often with disastrous results. It is now increasingly recognized that political meddling has consistently caused or worsened financial instability. . . . In East Asia in 1997–98, political interference in the regulatory and supervisory process postponed recognition of the severity of the crisis, delayed action, and, ultimately, deepened the crisis. In Korea, for example, a lack of independence impeded supervision. While the country's commercial banks were under the authority of the central bank (the Bank of Korea) and the Office of Banking Supervision, Korea's specialized banks and nonbank financial institutions were regulated by the Ministry of Finance and Economy. The ministry's weak supervision encouraged excessive risk taking by the nonbanks, which helped lead to the 1997 crisis. Korea subsequently reformed its supervisory system, both to give it more autonomy and to eliminate the regulatory and supervisory gaps.[106]

Ruth de Krivoy, former president of the Venezuelan central bank, commenting on the Venezuela banking crisis of 1994, cited ineffective regulation, weak supervision, and political interference as factors that weakened banks in Venezuela in the period leading up to the crisis.[107] She points out the need for lawmakers to "make bank supervisors strong and independent, and give them enough political support to allow them to perform their duties."[108]

---

[102] M. Quintyn & M. W. Taylor, *supra* n. 65, at 1.

[103] *See id.* at 1.

[104] *See id.*

[105] *See id.* at 2.

[106] *See id.* at 3.

[107] *See id. See also generally* R. de Krivoy, *Collapse: The Venezuelan Banking Crisis of '94* (Group of Thirty 2000); and, M. Da Costa, *Book Review of R. de Krivoy, Collapse: The Venezuelan Banking Crisis of '94*, 38(1) Fin. & Dev. J. (2001), http://www.imf.org/external/pubs/ft/fandd/2001/03/books.htm (accessed January 2, 2005).

[108] M. Quintyn & M.W. Taylor, *supra* n. 65, at 3.

In Indonesia, banking sector weaknesses stemmed from poorly enforced regulations and from the reluctance of supervisors to take action against politically well-connected banks, especially those linked to the Suharto family.[109] When the crisis hit, central bank procedures for dispensing liquidity support to troubled banks were overridden, it was claimed, on the direct instructions of the President.[110]

Even after Suharto's fall, political interference continued to undermine the bank restructuring effort.[111] The intrusive interventions of Indonesia's Financial Sector Action Committee, which was composed of several heads of economic ministries and chaired by the coordinating minister, undermined the credibility of the Indonesian Bank Restructuring Agency's work.[112]

In Japan, the lack of independence of financial supervisors in the Ministry of Finance weakened the Japanese financial sector and contributed to prolonged banking sector problems.[113] Although "there was probably little direct political pressure on the Ministry to allow weak banks to continue operating, the system lacked transparency, and implicit government guarantees of banking sector liabilities were understood to be widespread."[114] As a result, and given the declining reputation of the Ministry of Finance in the late 1990s, the Japanese Government created a new Financial Services Agency to oversee banking, insurance, and the securities markets, in part as an attempt to increase the independence of supervision.[115]

2.5   Arguments For and Against the Independent Regulator

Generally, it is well accepted that independent regulators can initiate market interventions shielded from political interference so as to improve regulatory and supervisory transparency, stability, and expertise.[116] However, is the concept of an independent regulator always good for the financial sector, and should a regulatory agency enjoy absolute independence?

In countries that are moving from a command economy, where financial markets and instruments are fairly weak, there might be good reason for the

---

[109] *See id.* at 3.

[110] *See id.*

[111] *See id.*

[112] *See id.*

[113] *See id.*

[114] *See id.*

[115] *See id.* at 4.

[116] *See id.* at 5.

government to intervene occasionally and strategically, for instance in cases that involve the threat of the insolvency of strategic firms. There, the State should be allowed, though only occasionally, to direct market forces as long as there is good cause for such intervention. By contrast, in countries that have well-developed financial markets and instruments, the financial sector may benefit more from absence of State intervention. The presence of a strong infrastructure and regulatory framework in these countries, including a culture where contractual rights are enforced, means that State intervention is not necessary for the market to function efficiently. Overall, there is increasing evidence from a number of countries suggesting that independent regulators have made regulation more effective, have led to smoother and more efficient operation of the market, and are a distinct improvement over regulatory functions located in government ministries.[117]

As we have already pointed out, the idea of an independent central bank provides an example of the success of such an independent regulator in fighting inflation. Since the late 1980s, more and more countries have freed their central banks from political control because evidence was growing that independent central banks are successful in achieving monetary stability—in other words, controlling inflation.[118] Making central banks independent frees them from political pressure and thus removes the inflationary bias that could otherwise unsettle monetary policy.[119]

Although the IMF argues that the disincentives for politicians to rescue failing banks, for example, are similar to those for government inaction in the face of inflation, in that the decision to close a failing bank is usually unpopular,[120] in some developing countries—especially those that are heavily dependent on one segment of the financial sector—there might be good cause, after identifying the role the State can play in the process of privatization, commercialization, or winding up of a State bank to allow for some degree of State intervention or participation. In such countries, although government subsidies to support the running of a State bank often lead to high fiscal costs, the ill-conceived privatization or liquidation of the State bank can also lead to high social costs, such as unemployment where the State bank has been a major employer. There is need, therefore, to consider the role of the State and any other mitigating factors, such as the use of employee share-ownership schemes, while factoring in the social costs that could result if privatization is not handled properly.

A common argument against the whole idea of an independent financial services regulator is that such agencies tend to respond to the wishes of the

---

[117] *See id.*

[118] *See id.* at 4.

[119] *See id.*

[120] *See id.*

best-organized interest groups.[121] It has been argued, for example, that:

> When regulators are free from political control, the risk of "regulatory cap-
> ture" by other groups—in particular, the industry they regulate—grows.
> Agencies that suffer from such capture come to identify industry interests
> (or even the interests of individual firms) with the public interest. And
> industry capture can undermine the effectiveness of regulation just as polit-
> ical pressure can.[122]

Where there is industry capture, regulators may, for example, formulate rules
so as to minimize industry costs rather than strike an appropriate balance between
those costs and public benefits.[123] They may also apply rules inconsistently and
exempt individual firms from certain requirements.[124]

In evaluating the merits and demerits of an independent regulator, it could be
useful to ask the following questions:

- In a country that does not have a well-developed and longstanding tradition
  of, e.g., banking supervision, why should a banking supervisory agency
  place a high premium on independence when there is not yet the institutional capacity and critical mass to deliver efficiently? Would not such an
  agency be more effective if it were to work in liaison with the government
  to find ways to improve its supervisory capacity first?
- In countries with relatively weaker economies, how financially independent should a regulator be, especially if the agency has just been established
  and requires substantial financial resources to get its work off the ground?
  Where will the resources come from?
- In a young and emerging economy, with a new stock market (financed by
  the State budget and the international donor community), for example, how
  far from the Government's national development agenda can the regulator
  stray in its policy for the development of the securities market?

These are some of the thorny issues that confront financial sector experts in
designing models of financial services regulation. In sum: Should a regulator be
absolutely independent? What does "absolute independence" mean? Or should
the independence of a regulator be incremental, tracking the development of the
financial market and business conduct in that market? It appears plausible to

---

[121] *See id.* at 5.

[122] *See id.* at 5–6.

[123] *See id.* at 6.

[124] *See id.*

argue that the concept of an independent regulator is relative and best understood by measuring independence against the yardstick of accountability and the degree of development of the financial sector as well as the regulator itself.

Another argument against the idea of an independent regulator, then, relates to the accountability of the regulator. An independent regulator might pursue an agenda of its own, going against the wishes of the political majority.[125] If this were to happen, the policy objectives of the government for the soundness of the financial services industry might not be carried out fully. Some commentators have branded independent regulatory agencies the "fourth branch of government," implying that they are outside the control of the traditional three branches that keep mature democratic systems in equilibrium through a system of checks and balances.[126] Quintyn and Taylor observe that, although such fears appear to be exaggerated, they nevertheless demonstrate the importance of having proper forms of accountability to balance the disadvantages of agency independence.[127]

It could be argued that achieving both independence from the industry regulated and political independence is as important as ensuring that the independent regulator is accountable. Quintyn and Taylor, however, argue that political independence remains the prime concern from the point of view of financial stability, given the vested interests that many national governments still have in the banking system—and therefore in bank regulation—as well as the dismal track record of political independence in supervisory arrangements.[128]

2.6 Conclusion

This chapter has examined the idea of promoting the independence of a financial services regulator as a corollary to the development of an efficient and effective regulatory framework for financial services supervision. The chapter examined different aspects of *independence* with a view to showing that law reform professionals, policy makers, and institutions concerned with the development of the law should indeed concern themselves with the independence of financial services regulators. The chapter highlighted the key features of a modern regulatory framework that enhance the independence of a regulator. Fundamental questions were raised regarding the independence of a financial services regulator: whether independence would necessarily guarantee quality regulation, and whether the mere fact that a financial services regulator is independent would prevent a financial crisis.

---

[125] *See id.*

[126] *See id.*

[127] *See id.*

[128] *See id.*

It was argued that the concept of an independent regulator is not only relative but that it is best understood by measuring independence against the yardstick of accountability and the degree of development of the financial sector and the regulator itself. Also, it was observed that although the concept of an independent regulator provides incentives for enhanced quality in regulation, the independence of a regulator may not necessarily prevent a financial crisis. The cardinal point discussed in the chapter is that achieving both political independence and independence from the industry regulated is as important as ensuring that the independent regulator is accountable.

CHAPTER 3

The Concept of a Unified
Financial Services Regulator

3.1 Introduction

This chapter examines the concept of a unified financial services regulator, highlighting differences in the approaches taken by different countries. The first part of the chapter explains the difference between a *partially* unified regulator and a *fully* unified regulator, fleshing out the obstacles and challenges different countries have faced in implementing models of unified financial services regulation. The second part endeavors to inform both policy and practice choices, examining issues and themes in the contemporary debate on unified financial services supervision. Then, examples of unified financial services supervision are laid out, showing the divergences in practice and approaches to structuring a unified regulator. The chapter concludes by reviewing a World Bank study so as to highlight lessons learned about unified financial services supervision and the value this book can add to the debate.

In many countries, the unified regulator is structured on either a functional or a silos matrix, depending on local conditions and the objectives of regulation.[129] As noted in Chapter 1, where departments of a regulatory agency, such as the Legal, Licensing, Supervision, and Investment Policy Departments, deal with different financial services and products across the financial sector without segregating these services and products on the basis of the type of business activity or the type of institution offering them, the regulator is said to be organized along functional lines. To illustrate, in a functional matrix, the Licensing Department would license insurance companies, securities firms, pension funds, banks, and all other financial intermediaries, including stockbrokers and collective investment schemes. By contrast, in a silos matrix a particular organizational unit would deal exclusively with the regulation and supervision of insurance, another would deal only with pension funds, and so on, with no crossing over into other areas of financial services. Here, although all supervisory functions are undertaken

---

[129] Here and elsewhere in the chapter, the word "regulation" can be substituted for the word "supervision," where the unified regulator has powers to both issue regulations and supervise financial services. Also, the word "regulation" can be used interchangeably with the word "supervision," depending again on whether the unified regulator has both powers.

by the regulator as a whole, insurance businesses are licensed and supervised separately from, say, securities firms or banks. The competing interests of various stakeholders can also have a bearing on the organizational structure of a unified regulator.

Another important distinction is that unification may be partial or full. Normally, where only two segments of the financial sector are supervised by a single regulator, as are pension funds and insurance companies in Zambia,[130] the regulator is said to be partially unified. Other examples of a partially unified regulator can be found when regulation of securities and insurance, banking and securities, or banking and insurance is combined. Any of these regulators may be housed within or outside the central bank, depending on a host of factors, such as the availability of office space, the availability of human and financial resources, and the objectives of financial services supervision.

A fully unified regulator will normally supervise all business activities in the financial sector, as does the UK's FSA. The structure and staffing of such a regulator is determined by such factors as where the regulator is housed and whether it undertakes prudential supervision only, conduct of business only, or both.

Assuming a country opts for a unified regulator, what does international experience tell us about the processes, obstacles, and approaches to establishing a unified regulator? Table 3.1, based on primary data, summarizes some answers to that question.

To further inform policy and practice choices, the next section examines the salient features of the debate about unified financial services supervision.

3.2   The Unfolding Debate

The academic debate about unified financial services supervision began in the late 1980s in the UK; it has now been joined by international organizations. Among the issues around unified financial services supervision confronting countries the world over are whether to establish a unified regulator and, if so, how to structure its institutional and regulatory framework. At the outset, it is important to point out that issues of regulatory organization are essentially second-order issues. Far more important—the first-order issue—is how to implement financial supervision, in particular supervisory capacity, and its quality and the soundness of the legal framework for supervision.

Over the years, financial supervision has often been organized, silo style, around specialist agencies that have separate responsibilities for banking, securities, and insurance sectors, but in recent years there has appeared a trend

---

[130] *See generally* below.

TABLE 3.1

Structuring Unified Regulators: Processes and Obstacles

Country	Separation of Regulation from Supervision	Independence of Regulatory Agency	Accountability
Latvia	Both functions done by the unified agency	Reasonably independent CEO and deputy appointed through Parliament Autonomous statutory institution Financed from market levies	Annual audits filed with Parliament
United Kingdom	Both functions done by the unified agency	Reasonably independent Company limited by guarantee Financed from market levies	Internal audit, providing accountability to the FSA Board and Executive
Norway	Regulations often laid down by Ministry of Finance and the King Supervision undertaken by unified agency	Statutory body: The King appoints the CEO and the deputy CEO, raising questions of the political independence of the agency Also, the King appoints the entire Board, and there is considerable Ministry of Finance involvement in administration Funded from market levies	Annual reporting on activities to the appropriate Ministry
Hungary	Both functions largely done by the unified agency	Statutory body Independence not well developed: Prime Minister nominates CEO and Deputy CEO, then Parliament appoints Largely funded from market levies	Annual reporting to both Parliamentary Committee and Government

(Table continues on the following page.)

TABLE 3.1 *(continued)*

Country	Separation of Regulation from Supervision	Independence of Regulatory Agency	Accountability
Korea	Both functions done by the unified agency	Statutory body, FSS (Financial Supervisory Services), is fairly independent. The Chairman of FSC (Financial Supervisory Commission) is the Governor of FSS, and FSC appoints senior officers of FSS FSS auditor is appointed by President Funded from market levies	FSS is accountable to FSC and SFC (Securities and Futures Commission)
Jamaica	Both functions done by the unified agency	Statutory body Reasonably independent regulator; appoints its own CEO Funded partially from parliamentary allocations and from market levies	Reports to the Minister within 90 days of the supervisory examination
Finland	Both functions done by the unified agency	Statutory body Reasonably independent; works closely with the central bank However, there are a number of politicians (e.g., three deputy ministers) on its Board Funded mainly from market levies	Presents an annual report to the Parliamentary Supervisory Council

Source: Compiled by this author, based on information provided by regulatory agencies and an assessment of country laws and regulations.

toward restructuring financial supervision into unified regulatory agencies—agencies that supervise two or more of these areas. A number of commentaries have been written on unified financial services supervision, discussing its advantages and disadvantages.[131]

Several economic scholars have advanced arguments for the advantages of a unified model.[132] The arguments relate to such factors as the economies of scale and scope that arise because a single regulator can take advantage of a single set of central support services; increased efficiency in allocation of regulatory resources across both regulated firms and types of regulated activities; the ease with which the unified regulator can resolve efficiently and effectively the conflicts that inevitably emerge between the different objectives of regulation; the avoidance of unjustifiable differences in supervisory approaches and the competitive inequalities imposed on regulated firms when multiple specialist regulators have inconsistent rules; and, where a unified regulator is given a clear set of responsibilities, the possibility of increased supervisory transparency and accountability.[133]

What are some of the preconditions for establishing a unified regulator? These are among the decisive factors:

- Sound and sustainable macroeconomic policies
- The necessary political will among stakeholders

---

[131] *See, for example,* the bulk of the literature reviewed in *International Developments Parts I* and *II, supra* n. 1; and K. K. Mwenda, *supra* n. 1.

[132] *See, for example, supra* nn. 113–16.

[133] *See generally* C. Briault, *The Rationale for a Single National Financial Services Regulator,* Occasional Paper Series No. 2 (Financial Services Authority May 1999). In another paper, Briault (*see* C. Briault, *A Single Regulator for the UK Financial Services Industry,* Financial Stability Review [November 1998]) observes that the benefits of a unified regulator include

- the harmonization, consolidation, and rationalization of the principles, rules, and guidance issued by existing regulators or embedded within existing legislation, while recognizing that what is appropriate for one type of business, market, or customer may not be appropriate for another;
- a single process for the authorization of firms and for the approval of some of their employees, using standard processes and a single database;
- a more consistent and coherent approach to risk-based supervision across the financial services industry, enabling supervisory resources and the burdens placed on regulated firms to be allocated more effectively and efficiently on the basis of the risks facing consumers of financial services;
- a more consistent and coherent approach to enforcement and discipline, while recognizing the need for appropriate differentiation; and
- in addition to a single regulator, single schemes for handling consumer complaints and compensation, and a single independent appeals tribunal.

See also M. Taylor & A. Fleming, *Integrated Financial Supervision: Lessons from Northern European Experience,* Policy Research Working Paper 2223 11 (World Bank 1999).

- Cooperation and sharing of information among financial services regulators as a country moves toward a single unified regulator
- Skilled human capital to support establishment and operation of the unified regulator
- Financial resources to support establishment and operation of the unified regulator
- Conglomerates and cross-ownership of groups of companies that pose risk of contagion during a financial crisis and are thus a good case for a unified regulator
- The practice of universal banking, also a good case for a unified regulator
- The interconnectedness of segments of the financial sector, assuming it has reached a minimum level of sophistication
- The emergence of new financial instruments and services from many segments of the financial sector
- The internationalization of best practices for unified financial services regulation
- A well-developed public infrastructure to support the establishment of a unified regulator
- Effective market discipline to provide similar support.

Generally, where there are both sustainable macroeconomic policies and effective market discipline, the presence of a well-structured framework for financial services supervision is likely to provide incentives to stimulate the conduct desired of market participants. Such a framework must be supported by sufficient operational and financial resources. Also, there must be effective enforcement of laws and regulations, avoiding at all costs politically motivated regulatory forbearance. In some developing countries, models of unified financial services supervision have been introduced that correspond with what is happening in the financial sector of some developed countries. In Europe, where the United Kingdom, Ireland, Germany, Norway, and Sweden have all set up unified regulators, the transition economies of the former Eastern bloc are now trying to imitate them, believing, of course, that this will help them gain quicker access to the European Union markets. From the point of view of the transition economies, such efforts constitute the internationalization of best practices.

Often, the establishment of a unified regulator is supported by the political will of major stakeholders. It is difficult to think of a buoyant and sound regulator that does not enjoy the support of its major stakeholders. If that were the case, even the enforcement of the law would be affected adversely: the lack of political will would undermine the legitimacy of the regulatory system, and enforcement of the law by demotivated policing parties would be lax.

To garner the political will of major stakeholders, the various financial services regulators should cooperate and share information as a country moves toward a single unified regulator. Also, the unified regulator should be staffed with people well qualified to carry out its functions.

Among the arguments making the case for a unified regulator is the view that unification can lead to economies of scale and scope within the regulatory agency. Also, a simplified single regulator can provide a system of operation that is more user-friendly to both regulated firms and consumers. Presented equally strongly are arguments postulating that establishing a unified regulator can mean introducing a regulatory structure that mirrors the business of regulated institutions and avoids problems of competitive inequality, inconsistencies, duplication, overlap, and gaps—the kinds of problems that can arise in a regulatory regime based upon several agencies. Models of a unified regulator have in many countries also been predicated on arguments that a mega-regulator can more rationally utilize scarce human resources and expertise, while also providing more effective accountability and reducing the costs imposed upon regulated firms (since they would need to deal with only a single regulator).

Meanwhile, others have pointed out possible shortcomings of the model; these include the possibility that a unified regulator may erode traditional functional distinctions between financial institutions and that it may not have a clear focus on the objectives and rationale of regulation (in other words, that it does not make the necessary differentiations between different types of institutions and businesses, such as wholesale and retail). There is also a fear that a unified regulator could lead to cultural conflict within the agency when regulators come from different sectors.

It is also argued that setting up a unified regulator may create an overly bureaucratic agency that has excessively concentrated power, posing the possibility that the risk spectrum among financial institutions may disappear or at least become blurred. Here, even the merits of economies of scale would be watered down where the unified regulator is seen as supervising almost everything under the sun and thus becoming monopolistic. Such an overwhelming "Christmas tree" effect can, in turn, lead to inefficiencies, such as bureaucratic red tape and possibly corruption if the regulatory and institutional framework does not provide for effective checks and balances.

Further, where there are other pressing matters to be dealt with in the economy, such as the resolution of a banking crisis, it might be ill-advised to rush into unifying regulatory agencies in the financial sector, unless unification is part of the overall strategy for resolving the crisis. Also, the transition to a unified regulator should be accompanied by appropriate systemic protections. In the UK, where there has been considerable academic and practitioner debate about the merits of an integrated model and where it has been argued that monetary and financial stability are related,[134] the following six themes have dominated the debate[135]:

1. The rapid structural change that has taken place in financial markets was spurred by an acceleration in financial innovation. This has challenged the assumptions behind the original structuring of regulatory organizations. There follows the question of whether institutional structure should mirror the evolution of the structure of the financial sector.

2. The realization that financial structure in the past has been the result of a series of ad hoc and pragmatic policy initiatives raises the question of whether—particularly in the wake of recent banking crises and dislocation—a more coherent structure should be put in place.

3. The increasing complexity of financial business, as evidenced by the emergence of financial conglomerates, has raised the issue of whether a series of agencies supervising parts of an institution can have a grasp of developments within the business as a whole.

4. The demands on regulation, and its complexity, have been increasing, in particular the surfacing of a need for enhanced regulation of "conduct of business," especially in the sale of financial products like pension schemes and consumer insurance policies.

5. Financial innovation is changing the risk characteristics of financial firms.

6. The increasing internationalization of banking has implications for the institutional structure of agencies at the national as well as the international level.

---

[134] *See* Taylor & Fleming, *id.* at 2. In that paper, Taylor and Fleming argue that: "An important issue in deciding to adopt a unified supervisory agency is to consider whether it should be concerned exclusively with prudential [that is, safety and soundness] regulation, or whether it should also have responsibility for conduct of business. . . . [It] should be noted only the United Kingdom, of the countries surveyed, has created a unified regulator with both prudential and conduct of business responsibilities."

[135] *See* Taylor & Fleming, *id.* at 3. *See also generally* C. A. E. Goodhart, P. Hartman, D. T. Llewellyn, L. Rojas-Suarez & S. Weisbrod, *Financial Regulation* (Routledge 1998); M. Taylor, *Twin Peaks: A Regulatory Structure for the New Century* (Centre for the Study of Financial Innovation 1995); M. Taylor, *Peak Practice: How to Reform the United Kingdom's Regulatory System* (Centre for the Study of Financial Innovation 1996); C. A. E. Goodhart, *The Costs of Regulation,* in *Financial Regulation or Over-Regulation* (A. Sheldon ed., Institute of Economic Affairs 1988); and C. Briault, *The Rationale for a Single National Financial Services Regulator, supra* n. 133.

This chapter, building on the ongoing debate,[136] takes stock of various developments relating to the organization of unified regulatory agencies. It seeks to provide perspectives on structural issues confronting unified regulators in different parts of the world.

3.3   Examples of Unified Regulators

3.3.1   Bulgaria

Bulgaria established a unified regulator for nonbanking financial services only, the Financial Supervisory Commission (FSC), on March 1, 2003.[137] Bulgaria's FSC was set up pursuant to the Financial Supervision Commission Act 2003.[138] Primary motivations for setting up the FSC were the increased consolidation of financial markets in the country; the overlap of activities of investment funds, insurance companies, pension funds, and some banking institutions; and the emergence of new financial institutions and products. To a large extent, all these reflected developments in Western Europe.[139] Today, the FSC is structured as a silos matrix. Its regulatory and supervisory functions are undertaken by three specialized divisions: Investment Supervision, Insurance Supervision, and Social Insurance Supervision.[140] The structure of these divisions has been adapted to

---

[136]*See for example*: Taylor & Fleming, *id.* at 1; R. K. Abrams & M. Taylor, *Issues in the Unification of Financial Sector Supervision*, IMF Operational Paper MAE/00/03 (IMF, Monetary and Exchange Affairs Dept. 2000); D. T. Llewellyn, *Introduction: The Institutional Structure of Regulatory Agencies*, in *How Countries Supervise Their Bank, Insurers and Securities Markets* (Central Banking Publications 1999); L. Sundararajan, A. Petersen, & G. Sensenbrenner, *Central Bank Reform in the Transition Economies* (IMF 1997); C. A. E. Goodhart, P. Hartman, *et al.*, *id.*; Taylor, *Twin Peaks*, *id*; Taylor, *Peak Practice*, *id.*; Goodhart, *id.*; Briault, *Rationale*, *supra* n. 133; D. T. Llewellyn, paper presented at the conference on Regulation and Stability in the Banking Sector, *Some Lessons for Bank Regulation from Recent Cases* (De Nederlandsche Bank, Amsterdam, November 3–5, 1999); Mwenda, *supra* n. 72; B. Drees & C. Pazarbasioglu, *The Nordic Banking Crisis: Pitfalls in Financial Liberalisation?* Occasional Paper 161 (IMF 1998); C. Lindgren, *Authorities' Roles and Organizational Issues in Systemic Bank Restructuring*, Working Paper WP/97/92-EA (IMF 1997); M. Blair, R. Cranston, C. Ryan & M. Taylor, *Blackstone's Guide to The Bank of England Act 1998* (Blackstone Press Limited 1998); Briault, *A Single Regulator*, *supra* n. 133; and Bartolini, *The Financial Services Authority: Structure, Mandate, and Policy Issues*, in Samiei, *et al.*, *supra* n. 77.

[137] *See generally* below.

[138] Financial Supervision Commission Act 2003 of Bulgaria, Articles 1(1) and 2(1).

[139] Financial Supervision Commission of Bulgaria, "About the Commission," http://www.fsc.bg/e_fsc_page.asp?v=2 (accessed April 15, 2004).

[140] *See id.*

FSC's major roles, which are the issuance of licenses and the carrying out of examinations.[141] The Insurance Supervision Division comprises the following three directorates: Regulatory Regimes and Consumer Protection; Inspections and Financial Supervision; and Regulatory Policy and Analysis. The Social Insurance Supervision Division consists of two directorates, the Regulatory Regimes and Risk Evaluation Directorate, and the Control Activities Directorate.[142] The Investment Supervision Division comprises the following three directorates: Regulatory Regimes; Supervision and Procedural Representation; and Market Analyses.

The Bulgarian FSC considers itself an independent body that is not influenced by the executive arm of the State.[143] Functionally, FSC reports to the National Assembly and operates as a specialized government body for regulation of the nonbanking financial sector,[144] carrying out functions that were previously the domain of the former State Securities Commission, the State Insurance Supervision Agency, and the Insurance Supervision Agency.[145] The primary functions of FSC are to facilitate, through legal, administrative, and informational means, and to maintain stability and transparency in, the investment, insurance, and social insurance markets.[146]

3.3.2   Zambia and Jamaica

The Zambian model of unified financial services supervision is unique.[147] Zambia has a twin system of unified financial services supervision: on the one hand, the Central Bank of Zambia (BOZ) has separate departments to supervise banks and nonbanking financial institutions; on the other, the Pensions and Insurance Authority (PIA) is responsible for supervising insurance companies and pension funds, even though both are in essence nonbanking financial institutions not that much different from those supervised by BOZ. One possible explanation for the anomaly could be that, under section 2 of the Banking and Financial Services Act of 1994, pension funds and insurance companies are not recognized as financial institutions that carry on "financial services business other than banking

---

[141] *See id.*

[142] *See id.*

[143] *See id.*

[144] *See id.*

[145] *See id.*

[146] *See id.*

[147] *See generally* K. K. Mwenda, *Unified Financial Services Supervision in Zambia: The Legal and Institutional Frameworks*, 36 Zambia L. J. 67–110 (2004), in which the efficiency of this model is examined in greater detail.

business." Another plausible argument is that the relevant department of BOZ is concerned only with the regulation and supervision of nonbanking financial institutions that accept deposits taking or provide loans.

A comparison could be made here with the institutional and regulatory framework for financial services supervision in Jamaica:

> The Bank of Jamaica (BOJ) has supervisory responsibility for deposit-taking institutions licensed under the financial legislation administered by the Central Bank. This responsibility is discharged by the Central Bank's Financial Institutions Supervisory Division and covers commercial banks, merchant banks, building societies, and more recently credit unions following their designation as specified financial institutions by the Minister of Finance and Planning in 1999.[148]

The Jamaican unified regulator, the Financial Services Commission, established under the Financial Services Commission Act of 2001, has overall responsibility for the regulation and supervision of institutions "that provide non-deposit-taking financial services in connection with insurance, the acquisition or disposal of securities within the meaning of the Securities Act and units under a registered unit trust within the meaning of the Unit Trust Act."[149]

From a public policy point of view, the argument in favor of BOZ regulating Zambian nonbanking financial institutions that accept deposits and make loans is premised on the need to protect the public should a nonbanking financial institution default.

3.4   Deciding Whether to Unify Financial Services Supervision

Should every country adopt a model of unified financial services supervision? The answer is a clear "no." Some countries would benefit from unification of only a few regulatory agencies. For example, the unification on April 1, 2002 of two agencies responsible for supervising pension funds and insurance businesses in Poland helped to strengthen regulation of financial services there.[150] Each country's framework must be structured with the objective of meeting the challenges of its own financial sector.

---

[148] Bank of Jamaica, *Supervision of Financial Institutions*, http://www.boj.org.jm/supervised_financial.php (accessed July 13, 2005).

[149] D. C. Walker, *The Powers of the FSC*, Jamaica Gleaner (Friday, June 22, 2002), http://www.jamaica-gleaner.com/gleaner/20020614/business/business7.html (accessed May 25, 2004).

[150] *See generally* Mwenda, *supra* n. 1.

What, then, is the ideal structure of a unified financial services regulatory agency? There is no rigidly fixed answer to that question. Different countries have taken different routes and approaches for a variety of reasons that may be, for instance, ideological, historical, economic, or political, or a combination thereof. Until there is a longer track record of experience with unified agencies, it is difficult to come to firm conclusions about their optimal structure. In some countries, for various reasons, some of them political, unification of all the major financial services regulatory bodies may be desirable. Yet that might not be appropriate in a country where in the financial sector there are limited connections among sector components or where there is no practice of universal banking or evidence of conglomerates. In countries where segments of the financial sector are well connected, there is a good case for moving toward unified supervision as the nature of banking and other financial services business evolves to encompass more complex and multifunctional operations.

3.5   A Contingency Approach

The discussion in this section shows that, though in the last few years a number of countries have moved to integrate different supervisory functions into a single agency,[151] how unified financial services supervision has been adopted and applied has varied from country to country. In approximately half the countries examined in a July 2000 study,[152] the regulatory structures were still based on specialist agencies, with banking, insurance, and securities each supervised by a dedicated agency[153] (see table 3.2). The other countries surveyed had combined elements of supervision into partially or fully unified supervisory agencies.

In a number of countries where separate supervisory agencies existed, the banking supervisor was the central bank, but this was not always the case.[154] In South Africa and the Slovak Republic, for instance, the securities and insurance sectors had a common regulator, while banks were regulated by a specialist agency.[155] Thus,

> the unified model is not as common as the recent attention it has received seem to suggest. The ten countries classified as having adopted this organizational form are Australia, Canada, Denmark, Iceland, Japan, Norway, the Republic of Korea, Singapore, Sweden, and the United Kingdom.

---

[151] Taylor & Fleming, *supra* n. 133, at 1.

[152] *See* Abrams & Taylor, *supra* n. 136. *See also, generally*, Llewellyn, *supra* n. 136.

[153] Abrams & Taylor, *supra* n. 136, at 6.

[154] *See id.* at 6.

[155] *See id.*

TABLE 3.2

Regulatory Structures in Selected Countries as of July 2000

Separate agencies for each main sector	35
Combined securities and insurance regulators	3
Combined banking and securities regulators	9
Combined banking and insurance regulators	13
Unified supervision (in central bank)	3
Unified supervision (outside central bank)	10

Source: Adapted from Central Banking Publications, *How Countries Supervise Their Bank, Insurer and Securities Markets* (Central Banking Publications 1999), as quoted in R.K. Abrams & M. Taylor, *Issues in the Unification of Financial Sector Supervision*, IMF Operational Paper MAE/00/03 6 (IMF, Monetary and Exchange Affairs Dept. 2000).

However, in at least two cases—Australia and Canada—the regulatory structure is not fully unified as securities regulation is conducted separately from banking and insurance regulation. Moreover, in Singapore's case, regulation has been unified within the central bank. This leaves only seven countries that have fully unified regulatory agencies separate from the central bank. Over half of these are in the Nordic countries. This observation may suggest that unified supervision has, to date, been a response to country-specific factors, and as such may not be universally applicable.[156]

3.6   Lessons Learned from Experience

Today, a number of countries are beginning to re-examine how their financial supervision is organized. While the observations just quoted are valid, there is some danger of viewing the cup as half empty when it might equally be considered half full. In fact, increased importance is being placed on the design of efficient and effective structures to support financial services supervision, and in some cases this is leading to partial or full unification. There is as yet no single right way of introducing or implementing unified models of financial services supervision. In Africa, for example, Mauritius has legislation that establishes a unified financial services regulatory agency. As the Mauritius International Financial Services Centre observes:

The Financial Services Development Act 2001 consolidates our existing regulatory and supervision frameworks while simultaneously putting in

---

[156] *See id.* at 7.

place a unified regulatory framework for the financial services sector. This new legislation also reflects changes made in line with initiatives of international bodies such as OECD, FATF, UN Offshore Forum and core principles of international supervisors. . . . The single regulatory framework has been achieved through a phased approach by the setting up of the Financial Services Commission on 1st December 2002 responsible for the licensing, regulation and supervision of the non-bank financial services and, at a later stage, after a review of the exercise to be carried out in three years' time, to the eventual integration of the Financial Services Centre with the Central Bank *i.e.* the Bank of Mauritius, into a single unified regulatory authority for the whole financial services sector[157]

Before the Mauritius Financial Services Development Act was enacted in 2001, regulatory oversight extended only to banking, insurance, securities, and offshore services, leaving certain sectors, such as fund management, pensions funds, leasing companies as well as financial intermediaries, partially or completely unregulated.[158] Yet the unregulated or partially regulated sectors are high-risk investment areas not only for depositors and investors but also for the stability of the entire financial system.[159]

In South Africa, as noted previously, the securities and insurance sectors have a common regulator, while banks are regulated by a specialist agency. In Nigeria, pension funds and some other financial services are supervised by the same regulatory agency, but the insurance business is supervised by a separate agency. Another African country that has a partially unified supervisory system is Zambia. While BOZ regulates financial institutions like banks, building societies, and *bureaux de change*, PIA regulates only insurance companies and pension funds and the Securities and Exchange Commission is concerned mainly with securities regulation. It appears that a good number of African countries are leaning toward partial unification.

In Europe, one commentator observed:

It is pleasing to see that throughout Europe there is a steady trend toward integration of one kind or another. As well as the UK, other European countries such as Germany, Netherlands, Belgium, Austria, Denmark, Sweden, Norway, as well as a number of the accession countries such as Estonia and Hungary have all moved to an integrated model of one kind or another.

---

[157] Mauritius International Financial Services Centre, *Financial Services Promotion Agency: Legislative Value*, http://www.mauritius-finance.com/legislate.html (accessed June 28, 2004).

[158] *See id.*

[159] *See id.*

Indeed, even the term "integrated regulation" is interpreted differently in different places. For example, in the UK we take it to mean the integration of all regulated financial services and to cover both Prudential supervision and the regulation of advice, sales and customer aftercare (what have traditionally been grouped together in the UK under the broad term Conduct of Business regulation). Other countries have integrated regulation of the different sectors, but have kept Prudential and Conduct of Business regulation separate. Indeed, I have heard some argue that there is an inherent conflict and contradiction between Prudential supervision and Conduct of Business regulation and that these cannot be solved within a single regulatory institution. I disagree with this point very strongly.[160]

Closely related to these developments in European countries, in Malta:

The MFSC [Malta Financial Services Centre] has been re-constituted as the Malta Financial Services Authority and its statutory functions are being revised to reflect its role as a single regulatory agency. It is not surprising that in the light of the huge new responsibilities placed on it, the MFSA's internal structures have had to be re-appraised. The 1994 reforms had left the original offshore authority MIBA [Malta International Business Authority] structure almost untouched. This may have been adequate for a small organization—at its peak, the then-MIBA had 24 employees. The current organization employs in excess of 120. Accordingly, the amendments provide a new internal architecture for the MFSA. A new Supervisory Council replaces the former Executive Committee, in place since 1989, as the regulatory arm of the new authority. This new Council is presided over by the newly created Director-General and groups the heads of all the regulatory units. The amendments safeguard full continuity between the MFSC and the MFSA and between the former Executive Committee and the new Supervisory Council. This guarantees the continued validity of all licences and actions issued or taken under the old structure. The transition will be entirely painless . . . The description of the functions of the Authority has been completely revamped. The MFSA has now been assigned a new strikingly explicit consumer protection orientation. Formerly this was only indirectly stated or implied. Now it is stated very specifically. The new Act has also established a new office for the specific purpose of handling of consumer

---

[160] *Integrated Financial Services Regulation: A Benchmark for Europe* 1–2 (CEA Conference, November 25, 2003), http://www.cea.assur.org/cea/v1.1/actu/pdf/uk/annexe 137.pdf (accessed May 25, 2004).

complaints in relation to financial services. A Consumer Complaints Manager "CCM", answerable to the Supervisory Council, has been appointed.[161]

In the case of the Philippines, Milo argues, financial services integration refers to the production or distribution of financial services traditionally associated with one of the three major financial sectors (banking, insurance, and securities) by service providers from another sector.[162] She notes that financial services integration can occur through the blurring of product lines because of innovation.[163] Similarly, for Germany, a report citing the German Minister of Finance spells out the following:

> The products and modes of distribution of banks, insurance companies, and securities firms are becoming more and more alike. In many cases, the distinctions are difficult to recognise, e.g., in the case of mortgage loans. In such cases, centralised supervision and equal treatment of equal risks are needed in order to ensure competitive neutrality. This can be achieved through the new integrated financial supervision. . . . There is a trend toward financial conglomerates in Europe which combine banks, insurance companies, and securities firms. . . . We must react to this development with an integrated and proactive supervisory system. The existing supervisory structure does not allow us to respond to the new risk scenarios posed by intersector combinations. The new integrated financial supervisory system can better protect the interests of investors and consumers.[164]

In Switzerland, a 2001 reports shows that Swiss banks threw their weight behind a government proposal to integrate the supervision of banking and insurance to ensure seamless regulation of the financial services industry.[165] It is expected that the merging of the Swiss Federal Banking Commission and the Swiss Federal Private Insurance Bureau into one agency will improve the flow of

---

[161] Malta Financial Services Authority, *Recent Amendments to Malta's Financial Services Legislation: A Review of Some Major Aspects of ACT no. XVII of 2002*, http://www. miamalta.org/MagSept02Page05.htm (accessed June 28, 2004).

[162] M. Milo, *Financial Services Integration and Consolidated Supervision: Some Issues to Consider for the Philippines, A Perspective Paper on Banking* (PowerPoint presentation, at 4), http://dirp3.pids.gov.ph/silver/documents/MSM%20presentation.pdf. (accessed November 18, 2004).

[163] *See id.* at 4.

[164] *First Experiences with Integrated Financial Market Supervision in Germany* (Gdańskiej Akademii Bankowej: Gdansk, Poland, 2003), p. 5, http://www.gab.com. pl/rn/materialy/2003/Volker_Henke.doc (accessed on May 25, 2004).

[165] Dawn (Internet edition), *Integrated Financial Supervision Favoured* (Thursday, February 1, 2001), http://dawn.com/2001/02/01/ebr12.htm (accessed May 25, 2004).

information and better reflect the trend toward consolidation in the industry.[166] In a public statement, the Swiss Bankers Association welcomed a suggestion from a group of government-commissioned experts that independent asset managers, called introducing brokers and foreign exchange traders, be adequately regulated; the association observed:

> All in all, we are convinced that the quality and reputation of Switzerland as a financial centre can be significantly strengthened by regulating financial intermediaries who have not been regulated until now.[167]

In the Pacific, Australia has a "twin peaks" model of unified financial services supervision.[168] In central Asia and the Far East, Japan, Korea, Malaysia, Pakistan, and Singapore are among the countries that have introduced unified financial services supervision.[169] In South America, a number of countries have prudential and market conduct regulation under one roof.[170] However, the Guatemalan, Venezuelan, Ecuadorian, Salvadoran, and Peruvian experiences have shown that even where a financial services regulator is in principle unified, it has tended to operate out of silos, with very little integration in practice.[171]

In Hungary, the unified regulator has been operating for some time now and, like its Icelandic, Maltese, and UK counterparts, it is a fully unified regulator of all financial institutions and markets. However, in Netherlands Antilles, Singapore, and Uruguay there is found a peculiar regulatory system where the central bank, not a separate regulatory agency, regulates securities firms and insurance companies as well as banks.[172]

Taking all this worldwide experience into account, it appears that if a country is to manage effectively the transition to a unified supervisory agency, a particularly important factor is the effective and efficient coordination of information among the major stakeholders, namely, the Ministry of Finance, the central bank, and the unified supervisory agency itself. Where there is an independent deposit

---

[166] *See id.*

[167] *See id.*

[168] The twin peaks model emphasizes the *objectives* of regulation: systemic stability and consumer protection. As Llewellyn observes: "The 'twin peaks' concept is based on a single prudential supervisory agency for all financial institutions (not only banks) and a single conduct of business (consumer protection) agency." *See* Llewellyn, *supra* n. 136, at xviii.

[169] E-mail from Jeffrey Carmichael, Chairman of the Australian Prudential Regulation Authority, to K. K. Mwenda, the author (June 3, 2001) (copy on file with author).

[170] *See id.*

[171] *See id.*

[172] *See* Llewellyn, *supra* n. 136, at xvii.

insurance agency and an independent payments and settlements clearing agency, they, too, must be consulted. Such coordination provides a useful risk control mechanism.

In a World Bank study, de Luna Martinez and Rose state that despite the intense debate on the advantages and disadvantages of integrated supervision, little is known about the experiences of countries that have adopted it and the obstacles and challenges they have faced in implementing it.[173] In an endeavor to respond to this call, this chapter provides original data on the obstacles and challenges faced by at least seven different countries—Latvia, the United Kingdom, Norway, Hungary, Korea, Jamaica, and Finland—in setting up unified regulators. The data confirms the thesis of this book, showing differences in the challenges faced by different countries. Because of these differences, there is not much evidence to suggest that there are broadly accepted best practices in the structural ordering of unified financial services supervision.

In their attempt to shed more light on the topic of unified financial services supervision,[174] de Luna Martinez and Rose present the results of a survey conducted in 15 countries that have adopted integrated supervision. They examine: (a) the reasons countries cited for establishing an integrated supervisory agency; (b) the scope of the regulatory and supervisory powers of these agencies; (c) the progress these agencies had made in harmonizing their regulatory and supervisory practices across the intermediaries they supervise; and (d) the practical problems policy makers faced in adopting integrated supervision.[175] They conclude that:

> The group of integrated supervisory agencies is not as homogeneous as it seems. Important differences arise with regard to the scope of regulatory and supervisory powers the agencies have been given. In fact, contrary to popular belief, less than 50 percent of the agencies can be categorized as mega-supervisors. Another finding is that in most countries progress toward the harmonization of prudential regulation and supervision across financial intermediaries remains limited. Interestingly, the survey revealed that practically all countries believe they have achieved a higher degree of harmonization in the regulation and supervision of banks and securities companies than between banks and insurance firms.[176]

---

[173] J. de Luna Martinez & T. A. Rose, *International Survey of Integrated Financial Sector Supervision*, Financial Sector Operations Policy Department, Policy Research Working Paper No. 3096, *Abstract* (World Bank 2003).

[174] *See id.*

[175] *See id.*

[176] *See id.*

The World Bank study identifies practical problems faced by the countries surveyed in establishing their unified agencies.[177] A number of findings in the World Bank study support the findings here[178] that we have yet to see the evolution of best practices in the field of unified financial services supervision.

3.7 Conclusion

This chapter has examined the concept of a unified financial services regulator, highlighting approaches taken by different countries in structuring their unified agencies. It has made the argument that in countries where segments of the financial sector are connected, there is a good case for establishing a unified regulator. In such countries, the nature of banking and financial services business is often developing to encompass more complex multifunctional operations.

It has been shown that, although unified financial services supervision has been adopted in a number of countries, its application has varied from country to country and there is no single right way of introducing or implementing specific models of unified financial services supervision. Experience so far seems to suggest that, in order for a country to manage effectively the transition to a unified regulator, a crucial factor is the efficient sharing of information among the major agency stakeholders in the supervisory system. Until there is a longer track record of experience with unified agencies, it is difficult to come to firm conclusions about the restructuring process and the optimal internal structure of such agencies.

---

[177] *See id.*

[178] As presented, for example, in Table 3.1 above.

CHAPTER 4

Frameworks for Unified Financial Services Supervision: Latvia, the Scandinavian Countries, and the United Kingdom

This chapter examines recent institutional and structural developments relating to unified financial services supervision in Latvia, the United Kingdom, and the Scandinavian countries.[179] After the concept of a unified regulator was introduced in Chapter 3, where approaches taken by different countries to structuring their unified regulators were examined, this chapter provides country studies of unified regulators in Latvia, the Scandinavian countries, and the United Kingdom.[180] The intent here is to place in context the preceding discussions of legal, policy, conceptual, and theoretical issues that affect the efficacy of the regulatory and institutional frameworks for financial services supervision. Similar studies of such countries as Canada, Germany, Poland, Iceland, Hungary, Zambia, and the Baltic States have already been undertaken.[181]

This chapter provides comparative perspectives on structural issues confronting financial services supervision in Latvia, the Scandinavian countries, and the United Kingdom. It consolidates the arguments that there is no strong evidence of international best practices relating to the structure of unified regulators and that until there is a longer track record of experience with unified agencies, it is difficult to come to firm conclusions about the optimal structure of such

---

[179] For some helpful background reading, *see also*: *International Developments Parts I and II*, *supra* n. 1; and K. K. Mwenda, *supra* n. 1.

[180] An earlier version of this chapter, coauthored by K. K. Mwenda & Judith M. Mvula-Mwenda, was published as a refereed article in the Murdoch University Electronic Journal of Law. *See* K. K. Mwenda & J. M. Mvula, *Unified Financial Services Supervision in Latvia, the United Kingdom and Scandinavian Countries*, 10(1) Murdoch U. Electronic J. L. (2003), http://www.murdoch.edu.au/elaw/issues/v10n1/mwenda101nf.html (accessed January 7, 2004).

[181] *See generally* K. K. Mwenda, *The Regulatory and Institutional Framework for Unified Financial Services Supervision in the Baltic States*, 9(2) J. East Eur. L. (2002); K. K. Mwenda, *Unified Financial Services Supervision in Zambia: The Legal and Institutional Frameworks*, 36 Zambia L. J. (2004); K. K. Mwenda, *Legal Aspects of Unified Financial Services Supervision in Germany*, 4(10) Germ. L. J. (2003); K. K. Mwenda, *supra* n. 1; *International Developments Parts I and II*, *supra* n. 1; and K. K. Mwenda & J. M. Mvula, *A Framework for Unified Financial Services Supervision: Lessons from Germany and Other European Countries*, 5 J. Intl. Banking Reg. (2003).

agencies. As a general rule, there is no hard and fast way or rigidly fixed answer to how to structure a unified regulator. Different countries have taken different routes and approaches. The varied reasons for these differences may be ideological, historical, economic, or political, or a combination.

4.1   Some Preliminary Issues

Countries contemplating a reorganization of their financial regulatory structure are confronted by two fundamental questions:

1. Should some model of unified financial services supervision be followed?
2. If unified financial services supervision were to be introduced, how should it be done?

It is important that countries address these questions with reference to their own economic, institutional, and political frameworks.[182] In some instances, reorganization of the regulatory structure may be ill-advised, for example where there are more pressing financial and economic issues. There is a question, for instance, as to whether countries facing imminent challenges in their financial sector, such as insolvencies among major banks, should be contemplating wholesale reorganization of the regulatory function when it might deflect attention away from the problems at hand.[183] In other countries, because there are very limited connections between the various segments of the financial sector (insurance, securities, pensions, and banking), maintaining the status quo may be more appropriate in the short term. Other countries may simply not have

---

[182] Taylor and Fleming state that "An important issue in deciding to adopt a unified supervisory agency is to consider whether it should be concerned exclusively with prudential [safety and soundness] regulation, or whether it should also have responsibility for conduct of business. . . . Only the United Kingdom, of the countries surveyed, has created a unified regulator with both prudential and conduct of business responsibilities." *See supra* n. 133, at 2. *Cf.* Goodhart, *et al.*, *supra* n. 135; Taylor, *supra* n. 135; Goodhart, *supra* n. 135; and Briault, *supra* n. 133.

[183] Addressing recent developments in bank regulation, Llewellyn draws an analogy and argues: "The causes of systemic bank distress are complex and multi-dimensional involving economic, financial, regulatory and structural weaknesses. This also means that regulatory approaches also need to be multi-dimensional. . . . An optimum 'regulatory regime' needs to incorporate seven key components: regulation (the rules imposed by official agencies), official supervision, incentive structures within banks, market discipline, intervention arrangements in the event of distress, corporate governance arrangements with banks, and the accountability of regulatory agencies. All are necessary but none alone are sufficient for systemic stability. As there are trade-offs between the components, regulatory strategy needs to focus on the overall impact of the regime rather than only the regulation component." *See* Llewellyn, *supra* n. 136, at Abstract.

enough financial resources and well-trained human capital to implement unified financial services supervision.

Assuming a country chooses to restructure its regulatory organization, what does the experience of other countries tell us about how unified financial services supervision should be introduced? The country studies set out below help to shed light on these questions.

4.2   The Latvian Model

As the chapter examines institutional and structural aspects of unified financial services supervision in Latvia, no attempt is made to delve into the policy foundation for introducing the model there. An insightful analysis of the reasons why many countries, including Australia, have turned to unified financial services supervision is contained in a separate discussion.[184]

To meaningfully evaluate the efficacy of the framework for unified financial services supervision in Latvia, it might be helpful first to examine some notable aspects of the Latvian financial, answering such questions as, how has the financial sector performed and what is the aim of unified financial services supervision in Latvia?

Generally, macroeconomic conditions in Latvia are favorable for a sustained and balanced evolution of the financial sector.[185] The country has been recovering steadily from the slowdown triggered by the Russian economic crisis. In 2000, for example, the real gross domestic product (GDP) of Latvia grew by about 6.5 percent, then in the first half of 2001 it grew by 8.75 percent. The growth was spurred primarily by exports and investment, though manufacturing, forestry, and services also showed strong gains.[186]

Notwithstanding the recovery of the Latvian economy in general and the banking system in particular, the latter remains susceptible to an array of potential shocks,[187] though as the IMF observes, none seem to pose significant risks. The most important stem from the rapid growth in lending and the associated

---

[184] *See International Developments Parts I and II, supra* n. 1. *See also* K. K. Mwenda, *supra* n. 1.

[185] *See* IMF, *The Republic of Latvia: Financial System Stability Assessment, Including Reports on Observance of Standards and Codes on the Following Topics: Banking Supervision; Payments Systems; Securities Regulation; Insurance Regulation; Corporate Governance; and Monetary and Financial Policy Transparency*, IMF Country Report No. 02/67 (IMF 2002), http://www.imf.org/external/pubs/ft/scr/2002/cr0267.pdf (accessed March 31, 2003).

[186] *See id.* at 11.

[187] *See id.*

competition among banks; the perception of possible money laundering; a possible increase in domestic interest rates; and the potential for exchange rate movements.[188] It is such factors on which are based the policy considerations for strengthening the structural framework for unified financial services supervision in a country like Latvia.

A further source of vulnerability in the Latvian economy may be the large proportion of nonresident deposits in Latvian banks.[189] The IMF estimates that in 2001 these deposits accounted for about one-half of total deposits in the Latvian banking system.[190]

> About one-half of the non-resident deposits are from the U.S., reportedly from Delaware-registered companies. Restrictive regulations in neighboring CIS countries are a factor in the attractiveness of Latvian banks for the non-resident businesses. Hence, there is a risk [that] both improved regulations and increased financial confidence in these countries may lead to a deposit outflow from Latvia, which may hamper the business prospects of those banks that are largely operating in CIS markets. While these deposits are usually invested in highly liquid OECD paper or redeposited abroad—with little maturity mismatch—the loss of this business could lead to a significant deterioration in profits, with possible systemic implications.[191]

Latvia is now well advanced in the transition process and many of the economic and financial issues that it confronts are those typical of a small open economy.[192] Further, most of the problems associated with the early stages of transition—the prevalence of the state in banking business, the persistence of state enterprises as a source of inefficiency, bad loans, and a weak credit culture—no longer pertain to Latvia.[193]

Although a number of privatizations remain to be carried out in Latvia, the enterprise sector is in an advanced stage of restructuring and there is now a firmer foundation on which to build the relationship of the regulator with the financial sector.[194] The banking sector—the largest component of the financial system of Latvia—has been greatly strengthened by the entry of foreign strategic

---

[188] *See id.*

[189] *See id.*

[190] *See id.*

[191] *See id.*

[192] *See id.* at 4.

[193] *See id.*

[194] *See id.*

investors.[195] Moreover, Latvia conforms to a large extent with most of the Basel Committee Core Principles for Effective Banking Supervision.[196]

Most of the insurance companies in Latvia are well capitalized and profitable.[197] The total capital and surplus maintained by the industry as a whole is approximately 3.5 times the amount required.[198] An IMF study found all the insurance companies examined in Latvia to be in compliance with the minimum standards of regulation.[199] Further, the insurance regulatory body of Latvia had adopted the solvency margin formula prescribed for member countries of the European Union. The insurance market in Latvia is not so strongly connected with the banking sector as to present a systemic risk to the financial system as a whole.

At present the few pension funds in Latvia do not represent a potential source of systemic risk either.[200] The Latvian stock market is both small and illiquid, and domestic institutional investors are only now beginning to emerge. Indeed, the absence of a more active securities market limits the private sector's borrowing options and concentrates funding risks within the banking sector.[201]

The structure of Latvia's financial sector as at December 2000 is illustrated in Table 4.1.

Although the number of companies operating in the insurance market in Latvia fell from 42 in 1992 to 25, in 2000 (8 life insurance and 17 non-life companies), a requirement that the companies maintain higher levels of minimum capital spurred consolidation.[202] By the end of 2001, life insurance companies were required to have at least LVL 2 million of base capital and non-life companies at least LVL 1 million.[203] The Insurance Supervision Inspectorate managed the consolidation process in an orderly manner, and there were no insolvencies that caused losses for policyholders.[204]

Generally, the domestic financial markets of Latvia are thin.[205] At the end of 2000, for example, government securities outstanding totaled LVL 226 million

---

[195] *See id.*

[196] *See id.* at 20.

[197] *See id.* at 17.

[198] *See id.*

[199] *See id.*

[200] *See id.*

[201] *See id.*

[202] *See* IMF, *supra* n. 185, at p. 8.

[203] *See id.* at 8.

[204] *See id.*

[205] However, the shallow domestic Lat market is balanced by the ability of banks in Latvia to access the Bank of Latvia's lending facilities. While the interbank market is the primary means of satisfying day-to-day liquidity needs, the Bank of Latvia provides backup liquidity support.

TABLE 4.1

Latvia: Structure of the Financial System at End-2000

Financial Institutions	Number	Assets	
		(millions of Lats-LVL)	(percent of GDP)
Banks	21	2,485	57.4
Credit unions	17	1	—
Insurance companies	25	115	2.7
Brokers	22	—	—
Pension funds	4	6	0.1
Investment funds	3	—	—
Leasing companies [206]	5	140	3.2

Source: Bank of Latvia, Insurance Supervision Inspectorate, and Securities Market Commission, as quoted in IMF, *The Republic of Latvia: Financial System Stability Assessment, Including Reports on Observance of Standards and Codes on the following topics: Banking Supervision; Payments Systems; Securities Regulation; Insurance Regulation; Corporate Governance; and Monetary and Financial Policy Transparency,* IMF Country Report No. 02/67, (IMF 2002), http://www.imf.org/external/pubs/ft/scr/2002/cr0267.pdf.

(about 5.25 percent of GDP).[207] The interbank market is also shallow, being concentrated in about five banks, one of which accounts for 25 to 30 percent of the market—a large enough position to move the market on its own.[208]

The interbank market for foreign exchange is significantly deeper, and thus:

> Commercial banks have access to lines of credit abroad, as approximately 70 percent of bank capital is foreign-owned. A result of these thin markets is volatility in money market interest rates. Commercial banks' liquidity forecasting is short-term with forecasts typically made for 3 to 6-month periods.[209]

---

[206] Of the five companies that undertake the bulk of leasing, three are subsidiaries of Latvian banks. Their assets are deduced from banks' assets (first row of the table). In addition, four banks undertake leasing activities in the order of Lat 85 million directly.

[207] *See* IMF, *supra* n. 185, at 9.

[208] *See id.* at 9.

[209] *See id.*

Today, the responsibility of supervising the financial sector in Latvia is vested in a unified financial services regulatory agency. The Financial and Capital Market Commission of Latvia started operating on July 1, 2001, in accordance with the Law on the Financial and Capital Market Commission adopted by the Latvian parliament in June 2000.[210] The Bank of Latvia observes:

> The experience of the Scandinavian countries has shown that as a financial market develops and its range of services provided expands, merging several financial supervisory authorities into one provides for more efficient supervision of the transactions in the financial sector, including an opportunity to assess market conditions more objectively and duly identify risk factors that could affect the interests of market participants and clients. . . . A unitary system for supervision of capital market has been successful in the Scandinavian countries, Australia, Canada, Japan, Korea, Singapore and Great Britain. Of the Central and East European countries, it has already been introduced in Hungary, and. . . Estonia.[211]

There has been a smooth transition from the Latvian supervisory agencies that separately regulated banking, securities, and insurance activities to a single unified regulatory body. The Financial and Capital Market Commission of Latvia merged the operations of the Banking Supervision Department of the Bank of Latvia, the Insurance Supervision Inspectorate in the Ministry of Finance, and the Securities Market Commission. The creation of a unified regulator was intended to enhance the stability and safety of the financial markets in Latvia.[212]

4.3   Structure of the Financial and Capital Market Commission

The Financial and Capital Market Commission (the Commission) in Latvia is organized mainly along functional lines rather than on a silos approach. The lead departments of the Commission focus on such functions as supervision and licensing, irrespective of the type of financial intermediary, institution, or business activity being supervised. Figure 4.1 illustrates the structure of the Commission.

---

[210] *See* Bank of Latvia, *On Establishing the Financial and Capital Market Commission in Latvia,* May 22, 2001, http://www.bank.lv/eng/main/sapinfo/lbpdip/index.php?30816&PHPSESSID=4560d09b0de5f4b291ea190bbc69477a (accessed February 18, 2003), copy on file with author.

[211] *See id.*

[212] *See* IMF, *supra* n. 185, at 19.

Figure 4.1. Structure of the Financial and Capital Market Commission

FCMC

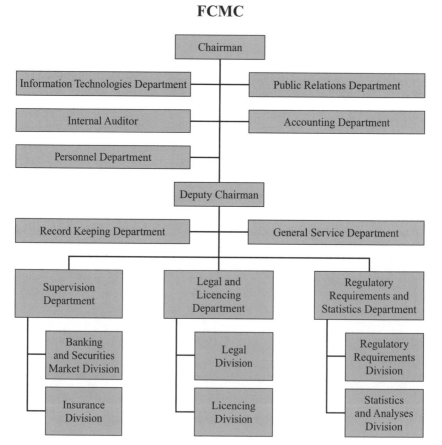

Source: Financial and Capital Market Commission Web site:
http://www.fktk.lv/fcmc/structure/ (accessed February 18, 2003).

The Commission has a staff of more than 90 people.[213] It has taken over from the Bank of Latvia the responsibility of supervising credit institutions, as well as the responsibilities previously held by the Deposit Insurance Guarantee Administration, the State Insurance Supervisory Inspectorate, and the Securities Market Commission.[214]

---

[213] A. Vanags, *Latvia's New Super-Regulators Have a Mission*, Transition Newsletter, http://www.worldbank.org/transitionnewsletter/octnovdec01/pgs35-36.htm (accessed February 18, 2003).

[214] *See id.*

4.3.1 Functions of the Commission

The Commission has the following functions:

1. To issue binding regulations and directives setting out requirements for the functioning of financial and capital market participants and the calculation and reporting of their performance indicators;
2. By controlling compliance with regulatory requirements and directives issued by the Commission, to regulate activities of financial and capital market participants; and
3. To specify qualification and conformity requirements for financial and capital market participants and their officials.[215]

The Commission is also responsible for establishing procedures for

- Licensing and registering financial and capital market participants
- Collecting, analyzing, and publishing information relating to the financial and capital market
- Ensuring accumulation of funds in the Deposit Guarantee Fund and the Protection Fund for the Insured
- Management and payment of compensation from the two Funds in accordance with the Laws on Deposits of Individuals and the Insurance Companies and their Supervision
- Analyzing regulatory requirements pertaining to the financial and capital market and drafting proposals for their improvement and harmonization with requirements of the European Union
- Engaging in systemic study, analysis, and forecasting of development of the financial and capital market
- Cooperating with foreign financial and capital market supervision authorities, and participating in relevant international organizations.[216]

In undertaking its functions related to financial and capital markets, the Commission can

- Issue regulations and directives governing activities of market participants
- Request and receive information necessary for the execution of its functions from participants

---

[215] The Law on the Financial and Capital Market Commission 2000, art. 6.
[216] *See id.*

- In certain types of cases, restrict the activities of market participants
- Verify compliance of market participants with legislation and the regulations and directives of the Commission
- Apply sanctions set forth when market participants (and their officials) have violated Commission requirements
- Participate in general meetings of market participants, convene meetings of market participant management bodies, and specify items for their agenda
- Request and receive free of charge, from the Commercial Register and other public institutions, any information it needs to execute its functions
- Cooperate with foreign financial and capital market supervision authorities and exchange information necessary to execute the functions specified by law.[217]

The Commission can also carry out other activities permitted under normative acts (subsidiary legislation) as part of the process of executing its statutory functions.[218] The regulations and directives issued by the Commission are binding on participants in the financial and capital markets.[219]

4.3.2 How the Commission Relates to Other Agencies

Under the Law on the Financial and Capital Market Commission 2000, the Commission and the central Bank of Latvia are required to share statistics relevant to the execution of their tasks,[220] but there is no equivalent requirement for the Commission and the Ministry of Finance to share information.[221] Nevertheless, at least once every quarter, the Commission is required to submit to the Bank of Latvia and the Ministry of Finance information summarizing the situation in the financial and capital market.[222] The Commission must also inform the Governor of the Bank of Latvia and the Minister of Finance, in

---

[217] *See id.* art. 7(1).

[218] *See id.* art. 7(2).

[219] *See id.* art. 8.

[220] *See id.* art. 10(3).

[221] In other countries, such as the United Kingdom and Hungary, the sharing of information between the unified regulator and other stakeholders in the financial system, such as the central bank, is facilitated by a Memorandum of Understanding. Generally, a Memorandum of Understanding, unlike a piece of legislation, is what some jurisprudents call "soft law."

[222] The Law on the Financial and Capital Market Commission 2000, art. 10(1).

writing, about the short-term liquidity problems of any market participant or any potential or actual insolvency of a market participant.[223] The Commission Law specifies that:

> *Article 11.* The Commission shall provide information on the financial status of specific credit institutions upon a written request of the Governor of the Bank of Latvia.
> *Article 12.* If not otherwise specified by regulatory requirements, the information referred to in this Section shall be considered restricted.

The Commission can also request that the Bank of Latvia extend a loan against collateral to any such institution.[224]

4.3.3 Management of the Commission

A five-member Council governs the Commission.[225] The members are the Chairperson; the Deputy-Chairperson; and three directors of Commission departments.[226] The Chairperson represents the Commission in its relations with state institutions, financial and capital market participants, and international organizations.[227]

Parliament appoints both the Chairperson and the Deputy for terms of six years each, based on a joint recommendation of the Minister of Finance and the Governor of the Bank of Latvia.[228] The Chairperson, in coordination with the Minister of Finance and the Governor of the Bank of Latvia, can appoint and remove other members of the Council.[229] Persons appointed to the Council, officers or not, must be competent in financial management and of good repute.[230] An appointee must also have at least five years experience in the Latvian financial and capital market.[231]

No person can be appointed who has a record of committing a "deliberate" criminal offense (whether the criminal record has been annulled or removed) or

---

[223] *See id.* art. 10(2).

[224] *See id.*

[225] *See id.* arts. 13(1) and (2). This 2000 law repealed the Latvian Law on Securities Market Commission (Zinotajs of the Parliament of the Republic of Latvia and the Cabinet of Ministers, 1995, No. 20; 1997, No. 14; 1998, No. 23).

[226] *See id.* art. 13(2).

[227] *See id.* art. 18(3).

[228] *See id.* art. 13(3).

[229] *See id.* art. 13(4).

[230] *See id.* art. 13(5).

[231] *See id.*

has been deprived of the right to engage in any type of "entrepreneurial activity."[232] The Commission Law does not, however, spell out what constitutes a "deliberate" offense; nor does it define "entrepreneurial activity." What is clear, though, is that Parliament can only dismiss the Chairperson or the Deputy Chairperson before term-end if:

1. The person has submitted an application to resign;
2. The person has been convicted of a criminal offense;
3. The person is not able to officiate for a period of six consecutive months due to illness or for any other reason; or
4. The Governor of the Bank of Latvia and the Minister of Finance have jointly submitted an application for early dismissal.[233]

However, it is not clear what the statutory grounds are for the Chairperson to remove other members from the Council; the Commission Law is silent on this. Also, while the law provides that the Chairperson of the Commission has power to hire and dismiss Commission staff,[234] it does not state the reasoning upon which such a decision is to be made. It is also not clear whether the Commission Law provides immunity to members and staff of the Commission from liability for acts or omissions done in good faith and in the course of business.

4.3.4   Meetings of the Council

Meetings of the Council are convened and presided over by the Chairperson of the Council or, during his or her absence, the Deputy Chairperson.[235] The quorum for a competent meeting is four members.[236]

Each member of the Council has the right to call a meeting of the Council by submitting a written application.[237] Meetings can be convened as needed, although they should not be held less often than once a month.[238]

The Council has power to pass resolutions by a simple majority. In cases of tie votes, the vote of the person chairing the meeting is decisive.[239] The Governor or

---

[232] *See id.* art. 13(6).

[233] *See id.* art. 14.

[234] *See id.* art. 18(2).

[235] *See id.* art. 15(1).

[236] *See id.* art. 15(2).

[237] *See id.* art. 15(3).

[238] *See id.* art. 15(4).

[239] *See id.* art. 16(1).

Deputy Governor of the Central Bank of Latvia and the Minister of Finance may participate in Council meetings as advisors.[240] Heads of the public organizations (professional associations) of financial and capital market participants may similarly take part in Council meetings, provided that the meetings have not been declared closed by resolution of the Council.[241] All members attending a Council meeting must sign its minutes.[242] The individual opinion of a member attending a Council meeting who votes against a resolution that passes is to be recorded in the minutes; that member will not be held responsible for the resolution of the Council.[243]

4.3.5 Powers of the Council

The Council of the Financial and Capital Market Commission has exclusive rights to:

- Approve supervisory and regulatory policies for the market
- Issue binding regulations and directives regulating the activities of market participants
- Issue special permits (licenses) or certificates authorizing operation in the market
- Suspend or renew the validity of the special permits (licenses) or certificates issued
- Annul any special permit (license) or certificate issued
- Decide on the application of sanctions against persons in breach of any of the requirements pertaining to the market.[244]

The Council may also:

- Specify fees to be paid by financial and capital market participants to finance activities of the Commission
- Approve the structure of the Commission and its structural units
- Approve the annual budget of the Commission
- Set compensation for Commission staff
- Approve the Commission's performance and annual report

---

[240] *See id.* art. 16(2).

[241] *See id.*

[242] *See id.* art. 16(3).

[243] *See id.* art. 16(4).

[244] *See id.* art. 17.

- Approve procedures for registration, processing, storage, distribution, and liquidation of information at the disposal of the Commission
- Pass resolutions on and sign cooperation agreements with the Bank of Latvia and foreign financial supervision authorities on the exchange of information necessary for supervision and regulation of the financial and capital market.[245]

4.3.6 The Consultative Council

A Consultative Council of the Financial and Capital Market Commission can be set up to promote efficiency in monitoring the financial and capital market and to promote the safety, stability, and growth of the market.[246] The Consultative Council would comprise representatives of the Commission and heads of the public organizations (professional associations) of financial and capital market participants.[247] Representation of public organizations is to be done on the principle of parity.

The Consultative Council is deemed competent to conduct business if at least half of its members are present at a meeting.[248] It can pass a resolution by a simple majority vote of the members present. In the case of a tie vote, the resolution is considered not to have passed.

Meetings of the Consultative Council are presided over by the Chairperson or Deputy Chairperson of the Commission.[249] The Commission is responsible for keeping a record of the deliberations of the Consultative Council, which is expected to be a collegial, advisory body, dealing with the following tasks:

- Reviewing legislation drafted for the regulation of the activities of participants in the financial and capital market
- At the request of a market participant and before consideration by the Commission, review the participant's complaints about the findings of a Commission inspection
- Prepare policy recommendations for the Council relevant to the execution of the Commission's statutory functions, and to improvement of the regulation and monitoring of the financial and capital market.[250]

---

[245] *See id.*

[246] *See id.* art. 21(1).

[247] *See id.* art. 21.

[248] *See id.*

[249] *See id.*

[250] *See id.* art. 21(1).

The Consultative Council is also responsible for issuing an opinion on the Commission's annual budget, submitting proposals to the Chairperson of the Commission regarding improvement of the Commission's activities, and supervising the accrual of funds with the Deposits Guarantee Fund and the Fund for the Protection of the Insured and the disbursement of compensation payments from these Funds. [251]

4.4 Strategic Goals of the Commission

The main strategic goal of the Commission is to ensure that there is overall stability in the financial and capital market of Latvia.[252] To achieve this stability, the Commission has promulgated the following objectives:

"1.1. Promotion of overall trust in the Latvian financial system. Currently the level of trust of the Latvian population in the financial and capital market is lower than the level achieved in the European Union (hereinafter, the EU). The Commission will focus its efforts on increasing the trust in the participants of the financial and capital market to the extent that the trust reaches or exceeds the level of trust observed in EU member countries.

"1.2. Surveillance of risks of the Latvian financial system. As the main goal of the Commission is to promote the stability in the financial and capital market, the Commission will devote a greater attention to the surveillance of risks faced by the market participants.[253]

The Commission postulates further:

"1.3. Minimisation of potential losses. One of the tasks of the Commission is to follow whether the market participants are able to meet their liabilities. The solvency of the market participants depends on economic and other factors. The [consultative] council, the board, and the largest shareholders of each market participant are responsible for the financial stability and activities of their firm in the market. Full responsibility is also born by the customers who are competent in financial issues, for instance, large enterprises and institutional investors. In order to minimise the risk of insolvency of market participants, the Commission will monitor the compliance with the requirements of minimum capital and capital adequacy, follow the activities of market participants, and will develop appropriate methodology for assessing the financial standing of market participants. The activities of

---

[251] *See id.*

[252] *See also* Financial and Capital Market Commission, at: http://www.latvianbanks.com/banks/Financial_and_Capital_Market_Commission.htm (accessed February 18, 2004).

[253] *See id.*

the Commission are aimed to minimize [sic] the impact of potential insolvency of certain market participants on customers' trust in the financial system of the country in general."[254]

The Commission has observed that among its objectives are (a) to reduce the possibilities that criminals will use the Latvian financial system to launder the proceeds of criminal activities; (b) to promote the security of information technologies; and (c) to promote the cost-effectiveness of the Commission's activities.[255]

Recognizing the necessity to ensure the quality of its supervision of the financial and capital market, the Commission also takes into account interests of participants in the financial and capital market in allocation of its financial resources. The Commission discourages the incurring of expenses not related to its tasks.[256]

Closely related to the objectives of the Commission are its strategic goals, which are to promote stability in the financial and capital market; promote development of the financial and capital market; and protect the interests of investors, depositors, and the insured.[257]

Apart from conducting prudential regulation and supervision, the Commission is expected also to strengthen public confidence and trust in the Latvian financial system.[258] Presently, the Latvian public has less trust than is generally true in EU members because there is a public perception that money is being laundered in Latvia.

The Commission is charged with fighting money laundering, promoting competition, and promoting public awareness of financial services and products, among a host of other tasks.[259] To promote the development of the financial sector, the Commission has promulgated three objectives:

1. Promotion of free competition in the financial and capital market
2. Promotion of financial innovations
3. Analysis and development of a viable taxation system.[260]

These objectives guide the Commission in its daily functions. The Commission maintains that development of the financial sector in Latvia should be

---

[254] *See id.*

[255] *See id.*

[256] *See id.*

[257] *See id. See also* Law on the Financial and Capital Market Commission 2000, art. 5.

[258] Vanags, *supra* n. 213.

[259] *See id. See also* Law on the Financial and Capital Market Commission 2000, art. 9.

[260] *See supra* n. 252.

supported by implementation of international accounting standards and the cooperation of the Commission with professional associations of market participants.[261] On the protection of interests of investors, depositors, and the insured, the Commission observes that it will "follow whether the participants of the financial and capital market provide to the customers of the financial and capital market highly qualitative . . . service corresponding to the norms of business ethics."[262]

4.5 Other Aspects of the Regulatory Framework

The Commission enjoys full rights as an independent and autonomous public institution.[263] Annually by July 1 it files with the Parliament of Latvia a written report on its performance in the preceding year, with complete audited financial statements.[264] For purposes of its responsibility of regulating and monitoring the activities of market participants,[265] Article 4 of the Commission Law defines "participants" in the financial and capital markets as "issuers, investors, credit institutions, insurers, private pension funds, insurance brokers, stock exchanges, depositories, broker companies, brokers, investment companies and investment consultants."

Though the Commission is required to make independent decisions within the limits of its authority, it is not clear whether its decisions can be challenged in a court of law on the grounds that the decision was not made independently.

The Commission is entrusted with powers to execute functions assigned to it by law and is responsible for the execution of these functions.[266] The Commission Law prohibits any interference with activities of the Commission, except by an institution or official authorized by law to intervene.[267] The 2000 statute is, however, not clear on the type of penalty that would be meted out to a party acting in breach of this prohibition.

4.5.1 Assets of the Commission

Pursuant to Article 3(1) of the Commission Law, the Commission is entitled to be assigned property owned by the state. It must also have an independent balance

---

[261] *See id.*

[262] *See id.*

[263] The Law on the Financial and Capital Market Commission 2000, art. 2(1).

[264] *See id.* art. 27.

[265] *See id.* art. 2(1).

[266] *See id.* art. 2(2).

[267] *See id.*

sheet. The Commission has a seal bearing its full name, is endowed with other corporate requisites, and has an account with the Bank of Latvia.[268]

4.5.2   Financing of the Commission

Activities of the Commission are financed by payments of participants in the financial and capital market in amounts specified by the Council of the Commission; these may not exceed amounts set by law.[269] This rule helps to promote the independence and autonomy of the Commission. Indeed, in many cases where a regulatory body is funded from the central government budget, its functional and operational autonomy is compromised. There is also the likelihood that the regulatory body will not have adequate political independence to carry out its duties effectively, given the weight of interference from the executive arm of the State.

We now examine developments relating to unified financial services supervision in the Scandinavian countries.

4.6   Unified Financial Services Supervision in the Scandinavian Countries

There is some variation among the models of financial services supervision provided by Scandinavian countries.

4.6.1   Norway

Norway was the first to move to a model for unified financial supervision.[270] In 1986, after a long process of consolidating its regulatory system, Norway merged its Banking and Insurance Inspectorates.[271] This development followed an experience of:

> having been influenced by broadly similar considerations in making the move toward an integrated approach to regulation and having reaped many of the same benefits from this approach. Chief among these benefits has been obtaining economies of scale in the use of scarce regulatory resources in comparatively small, highly concentrated financial systems in which financial conglomerate groups predominate. *[footnote omitted]*
>
> . . .

---

[268] *See id.* art. 3(2).

[269] *See id.* art. 22(1).

[270] Mwenda, *supra* n. 72, at 113.

[271] *See id.*

[Norway's] Bank Inspectorate could trace its history back to the end of the last century, when it was established for the supervision of savings banks. The supervision of commercial banks was added to its responsibilities in the 1920's. Banking supervision has thus never been formally part of the responsibilities of the Norwegian central bank, and hence the creation of a unified regulatory authority did not involve any significant dilution of the central bank's range of powers. Indeed, a proposal in 1974 for the merger of the bank inspectorate with the central bank was defeated in parliament. In 1983 the Banking Inspectorate further acquired some of the functions of the securities bureau of the Ministry of Finance.[272]

While the Ministry of Finance continued to be responsible for regulating the Oslo Stock Exchange,[273] the Banking Inspectorate was entrusted with powers to undertake prudential supervision of specialist securities firms and investment management firms.[274] Given that banks in Norway were already the most active participants in the securities markets, placing supervision of nonbank securities firms under the Bank Inspectorate was a natural extension of its role in overseeing nonbank securities activities.[275]

Since 1986 Norway's single regulatory agency, the Kredittilsynet, has regulated banks, nonbank investment firms, and insurance companies, giving primary attention to their solvency.[276] However, although the Norwegian regulatory agency is also responsible for regulating real estate brokers and auditing firms, it had by November 1999 still not been granted the formal authority to supervise the Oslo Stock Exchange.[277] The enactment if Norway's Stock Exchange Act on November 17, 2000, gave the Kredittilsynet the power to supervise the Oslo Stock Exchange.[278]

On the other hand, section 1 of the Financial Supervision Act, No. 1 of 7 December 1956, regulating the supervision of Norwegian credit institutions,

---

[272] Taylor & Fleming, *supra* n. 133, at 4–5.

[273] This is the only organized financial market in Norway.

[274] Taylor & Fleming, *supra* n. 133, at 5.

[275] *See id.*

[276] *See id.*

[277] *See id.*

[278] *See Guidelines for Co-operation between Oslo Exchanges and the Bank, Insurance and Securities Commission,* March/April 2001, at 3, available at http://gammel.ose.no/pdf/guidelines.pdf. *See also*, Norway's Stock Exchange Act 2000, section 8-1, dealing with "Supervisory Authority." Although the Oslo Stock Exchange is by law supervised by the Kredittilsynet, it is the Ministry of Finance that has statutory power, under section 2-1 of the Stock Exchange Act 2000, to authorize and license a stock market in Norway. Thus, in essence, the Act vests supervision of the Oslo Stock Exchange in an authority other than that charged with responsibility for licensing the stock exchange.

insurance companies, and securities trading, states, with numerous crossreferences to other statutes, that it deals with the supervision of

- commercial banks
- savings banks
- non-life insurance companies, including the general agents (principal agents) in Norway of foreign nonlife insurance companies
- life insurance companies, including principal agents of foreign companies
- branches of credit institutions, insofar as their activities in Norway are concerned
- finance companies and mortgage companies
- any person who is required, under the Financial Institutions Act, to notify the Kredittilsynet of organized or commercial intermediation of loans
- any undertaking falling within certain sections of the Financial Institutions Act or which the King excepts from any of the provisions of that Act when it is decided that the Kredittilsynet shall supervise the business
- auditors and firms of auditors approved under the Auditors Act
- maritime insurance associations
- representative offices in Norway of foreign financial institutions
- investment firms and other undertakings carrying on business connected with securities trading
- private, municipal, and county municipal pension funds
- other undertakings that may be specified by law.

A Board of five members manages the Kredittilsynet.[279] The King appoints members and deputy members of the Board;[280] its chairman and vice chairman;[281] and the director-general of the Kredittilsynet, who serves a six–year term.[282] The members and deputy members of the Board are appointed for four–year terms.[283] The King has powers to lay down instructions for the Board,[284] so it is not clear how much political independence and functional and operational autonomy the Kredittilsynet enjoys.

Two members are elected by and from among the employees to supplement the Board when it deals with administrative business.[285] The election arrangement is

---

[279] Norway's Financial Supervision Act 1956, sec. 2.

[280] *See id.*

[281] *See id.*

[282] *See id.*

[283] *See id.*

[284] *See id.*

[285] *See id.*

agreed upon by negotiation with the employees; if agreement cannot be reached, an arrangement is stipulated by the Ministry.[286] The Norges Bank has an observer on the Board who is entitled to speak and to submit proposals, but not to vote. The Ministry appoints the observer and a deputy for a period of four years, following a proposal from the Norges Bank.[287]

4.6.2   Sweden and Denmark

In Sweden, the Finansinspektionen, which is the institution charged with unified financial supervision, was set up in 1991.[288] As the Finansinspektionen observes:

> The Swedish Financial Supervisory Authority, Finansinspektionen, is a public authority. Our role is to promote stability and efficiency in the financial system as well as to ensure an effective consumer protection. We authorize, supervise and monitor all companies operating in Swedish financial markets. The Finansinspektionen is accountable to the Ministry of Finance.[289]

The Finansinspektionen monitors and analyzes trends in the financial market.[290] It assesses the financial health of individual companies, the various sectors, and the financial market as a whole.[291] Furthermore, the Finansinspektionen examines risks and control systems in financial companies and supervises compliance with statutes, ordinances, and other regulations.

In Sweden, business operations that offer financial services require a permit from the Finansinspektionen.[292] This unified regulatory body also issues regulations and general guidelines and assesses whether current legislation needs to be amended. It supervises compliance with the Swedish Insider Dealing Act and investigates suspected offenses and share price manipulations.[293] The Finansinspektionen also works to ensure that companies disclose complete and accurate information to their customers. Finally, the agency prepares rules for financial reporting by financial companies.[294]

---

[286] *See id.*

[287] *See id.*

[288] Taylor & Fleming, *supra* n. 133, at 7.

[289] *Finansinspektionen* (FI, the Swedish unified regulator), http://www.fi.se/Templates/ StartSectionPage____842.aspx (accessed July 13, 2004).

[290] *See id.*

[291] *See id.*

[292] *See id.*

[293] *See id.*

[294] *See id.*

The Swedish Finansinspektionen's counterpart in Denmark, the Finanstilsynet, was established pursuant to a merger of banking and insurance regulatory agencies in 1988.[295] Section 3(2) of the Danish Financial Business Act 2001[296] provides that the Danish Financial Supervisory Authority may lay down rules and guidelines on honest business principles and good practices. Where the rules and guidelines involve marketing and competition, the Danish Financial Supervisory Authority will carry out negotiations with the Danish Consumer Ombudsman and the Competition Authority of Denmark.

The responsibilities of both the Swedish and Danish regulatory bodies are similar to those of the Norwegian Kredittilsynet. In Denmark, as in Norway, the banking supervisory authority had enjoyed a long history as an agency outside the central bank and the prudential supervision of nonbank securities firms was

---

[295] Taylor & Fleming, *supra* n. 133, at 6.

[296] This statute implements Council Directive 86/635/EEC of 8 December 1986 on the annual accounts and consolidated accounts of banks and other financial institutions, OJ L 372, 31.12.1986, p. 1; Council Directive 90/618/EEC of 8 November 1990 amending, particularly as regards motor vehicle liability insurance, Directive 73/239/EEC and Directive 88/357/EEC, which concern the coordination of laws, regulations, and administrative provisions relating to direct insurance other than life assurance, OJ L 330, 29.11.1990, p. 44; Council Directive 90/619/EEC of 8 November 1990 on the coordination of laws, regulations, and administrative provisions relating to direct life assurance, laying down provisions to facilitate the effective exercise of freedom to provide services and amends Directive 79/267/EEC, OJ L 330, 29.11.1990, p. 50; Council Directive 91/674/EEC of 19 December 1991 on the annual accounts and consolidated accounts of insurance undertakings, OJ L 374, 31.12.1991, p. 7; Council Directive 92/49/EEC of 18 June 1992 on the coordination of laws, regulations, and administrative provisions relating to direct insurance other than life assurance and amending Directives 73/239/EEC and 88/357/EEC (third non-life insurance Directive), OJ L 228, 11.08.1992, p. 1; Council Directive 92/96/EEC of 10 November 1992 on the coordination of laws, regulations, and administrative provisions relating to direct life assurance and amending Directives 79/267/EEC and 90/619/EEC (third life assurance Directive), OJ L 360, 09.12.1992, p. 1; Council Directive 93/22/EEC of 10 May 1993 on investment services in the securities field, OJ L 141, 11.06.1993, p. 27; European Parliament and Council Directive 95/26/EC of 29 June 1995 amending Directives 77/780/EEC and 89/646/EEC in the field of credit institutions, Directives 73/239/EEC and 92/49/EEC in the field of non-life insurance, Directives 79/267/EEC and 92/96/EEC in the field of life assurance, Directive 93/22/EEC in the field of investment firms, and Directive 85/611/EEC in the field of undertakings for collective investment in transferable securities (Ucits), with a view to reinforcing prudential supervision, OJ L 168, 18.07.1995, p. 7; Directive 98/78/EC of the European Parliament and of the Council of 27 October 1998 on the supplementary supervision of insurance undertakings in an insurance group, OJ L 330, 05.12.1998, p. 1; Directive 2000/12/EC of the European Parliament and of the Council of 20 March 2000 relating to the taking up and pursuit of the business of credit institutions, OJ L 126, 26.05.2000, p. 1; and Directive 2000/64/EC of the European Parliament and of the Council of 7 November 2000 amending Council Directives 85/611/EEC, 92/49/EEC, 92/96/EEC and 93/22/EEC as regard exchange of information with third countries, OJ L 290, 17.11.2000, p. 27.

part of its responsibilities before a fully unified agency was created.[297] However, the creation of the Danish framework for unified financial supervision was "largely an administrative arrangement, and there was no fundamental review of legislation governing its supervisory activities at the time of the merger."[298] For this reason, the Danish unified regulatory body operates under a number of different statutes inherited from predecessor organizations.[299] Although Denmark made efforts to harmonize its legislation in the 1990s, governance of the Danish regulatory body has not been fully unified.[300]

In Sweden, the creation of the Finansinspektionen was prompted by the banking crisis that hit Sweden in 1990–91.[301] There was also a political desire to keep up with other Scandinavian countries that had already established a framework for unified financial supervision.[302] In addition, and apart from the fact that Sweden, unlike Norway and Denmark, is a member of the Basel Committee on Banking Supervision and thus more likely to be attracted to achieving economies of scale and enhancing its international presence, there is also a long history of enhanced links between the banking and insurance sectors in Sweden.[303]

By contrast, Finland has opted not to adopt a fully unified approach to financial supervision, though until the late 1980s the Finnish regulatory framework mirrored that of Norway, Denmark, and Sweden.[304] A number of institutional changes that were introduced to the Finnish system focused mainly on enhancing the link between banking supervisors and the Bank of Finland.[305]

It is against this background that the Finnish FSA was established. Section 1 of the Finnish Financial Supervision Authority Act 1993 provides that the Finnish FSA,

---

[297] *See* Taylor & Fleming, *supra* n. 133, at 6.

[298] *See id.*

[299] *See id.* For relevant Danish legislation, *see for example* the Consolidated Insurance Mediation Act, 2001; the Consolidated Insurance Business Act, 2002; the Investment Companies Consolidated Act, 2000; the Commercial Banks and Savings Banks, etc. Consolidated Act, 2001; the Mortgage Credit Act, 2001; the Danish Supervision of Company Pension Funds Act, 1999; and the Consolidated Act on Measures to Prevent Money Laundering and Financing of Terrorism, 2002.

[300] *See* Taylor & Fleming, *supra* n. 133, at 6.

[301] *See id.* at 7. *See also generally* Drees & Pazarbasioglu, *supra* n. 136, where it is argued that although the banking crises in Norway, Sweden, and Finland in the early 1990s followed a similar pattern and appear to have had similar causes, the impact on the structure of regulation differed significantly between Norway and Sweden, on the one hand, and Finland, on the other.

[302] *See* Taylor & Fleming, *supra* n. 133, at 7.

[303] *See id.*

[304] *See id.*

[305] *See id.* at 8.

operating in connection with the Bank of Finland, has powers to supervise financial markets and "entities" operating in the market. Separate statutory provisions apply to the supervision of insurance and pension institutions.[306]

Under section 2 of the act, "supervised entities" are

- credit institutions (cf. Credit Institutions Act)
- guarantee funds of a deposit bank; a deposit guarantee fund (Credit Institutions Act, chapter 6a)
- branches of a foreign credit institution
- representative offices of a foreign credit institution
- management companies and custodians
- investment firms
- investor compensation funds as referred to in the Investment Firms Act
- branches and representatives office of foreign investment firms
- stock exchanges
- options corporations
- market makers, as referred to in chapter 1, section 4 of the Act on Trading in Standardized Options and Futures
- clearing corporations and clearing parties
- central securities depositories, the fund of a central securities depository and the clearing fund of a central securities depository
- authorized book-entry registrars
- pawnshops
- cooperative societies as referred to in section 41a of the Cooperative Banks Act (1126/93)
- any amalgamation and central body of the cooperative banks, as referred to in section 7a of the Cooperative Banks Act
- holding corporations of a credit institution and an investment firm
- corporations holding a controlling interest in a stock exchange, options corporation, clearing corporation, or a central securities depository as referred to in chapter 1, section 5, of the Securities Markets Act
- holding companies of a financial conglomerate, as referred to in the Act on the Supervision of Financial Conglomerates, where the Finnish FSA is the coordinating supervisory authority of the financial conglomerate.

The Finnish FSA works closely with the Finnish Insurance Supervision Authority and other agencies that supervise financial markets.[307] Although administratively connected to the Bank of Finland, the Finnish FSA is independent in its

---

[306] Financial Supervision Authority Act, 1993, of Finland, sec. 1.

[307] *See id.* sec. 4(6).

decision making.[308] Nevertheless, the political independence of the Finish FSA remains to be seen, especially since the President of the Republic of Finland appoints the FSA director-general,[309] and members of the Parliamentary Supervisory Council have administrative duties to (a) appoint three members of the FSA Board and their personal deputies for three years at a time, on the basis of proposals by the Bank of Finland, the competent Ministry, and the Ministry responsible for insurance business; (b) appoint the chairman and the deputy chairman of the Board, and, on the basis of a proposal by the Board, a deputy to the director-general; (c) decide upon bases for setting the director-general's salary, leave of absence, and annual leave; (d) decide upon reprimanding the director-general and on other matters related to the employment relationship; and (e) confirm FSA rules of procedure on the basis of a proposal by the Board.[310]

Contrasting the model for unified financial supervision in many Scandinavian countries with that in the UK, it can be argued:

> For different reasons, the United Kingdom's adoption of unified regulation stands out as something of an exception among northern European countries. Unlike the Scandinavian countries, the UK is home to an international financial centre and its domestic financial services industry is much larger, more diverse and less concentrated than in Scandinavia. Furthermore, the UK's Financial Services Authority is responsible for both prudential and conduct of business regulation, unlike its counterparts in Scandinavia which have focused on prudential regulation only. . . . Finally, the formation of the UK Financial Services Authority has been undertaken as a radical, "Big Bang" measure, bringing together nine existing regulatory bodies. By contrast, the Scandinavian integrated regulators were the product of a long process of agency consolidation, and were formed primarily from the merger of banking and insurance inspectorates . . . the growth of bancassurance business [that is, financial conglomerate groups combining both banking and insurance activities] was regarded as a powerful reason for adopting an integrated approach to supervision [in most Scandinavian countries]. . . . None of the three Scandinavian integrated regulatory bodies [in Sweden, Norway, and Denmark] was created by removing the banking supervision function from the central bank: in each case the regulation of commercial banks had long been conducted by a specialist banking supervisory body.[311]

---

[308] *See* Taylor & Fleming, *supra* n. 133, at 8.

[309] Financial Supervision Authority Act, 1993, of Finland, sec. 8.

[310] *See id.* sec. 5.

[311] *See* Taylor & Fleming, *supra* n. 133, at 9 and 17.

4.7 Unified Financial Services Supervision in the United Kingdom

In the UK, the Bank of England Act 1998 transferred banking supervision from the Bank of England to the Financial Services Authority.[312] Until then, the legal pedigree for powers of the Bank to conduct financial services supervision rested not only in the Banking Act 1987 but also in section 101(4) of the Building Societies Act 1986 and in the Banking Coordination (Second Council Directive) Regulations 1992. Under these laws, the core responsibilities of the Bank of England related to monetary stability, monetary analysis, monetary operations, banking activities, financial stability, and supervision and surveillance. Today powers to supervise banks, listed money market institutions (as defined in section 43 of the Financial Services Act 1986[313]), and related clearing houses (as defined in section 171 of the Companies Act 1989) now rest with the Financial Services Authority.[314] Under section 153 of the Financial Services and Markets Act 2000, the Authority has power to exercise its rule-making powers in writing.

The institutional and regulatory framework set up by the Bank of England Act 1998 endeavors, *inter alia*, to balance the roles of the Bank and of the Treasury. As Blair observes:

> This aspect is the one that has attracted the greatest amount of public attention. So far as the law is concerned, section 10 removes from the Treasury the power to give directions to the Bank in relation to monetary policy. That said, the Treasury have . . . important powers to condition the general strategy in relation to monetary policy. Critically, section 12 enables the Treasury to specify what price stability is to be taken to consist of, and what the government's economic policy is to be taken to be. These are the two elements, and the only two elements, of the Bank's statutory objectives in relation to monetary policy, though the second of them contains a subsidiary reference to objectives for growth and employment.[315]

In general, the areas expected to be influenced by enactment of the Bank of England Act 1998 are the stability of the financial system as a whole and of the

---

[312] *See* Bank of England Act 1998, Section 21. It is important to delineate clearly the roles of any other supervisory authority so as to avoid the potential for conflicts of interest. For further readings *see* C. Lindgren, *Authorities' Roles and Organizational Issues in Systemic Bank Restructuring,* Working Paper WP/97/92-EA (IMF 1997).

[313] Repeal of this act is being considered.

[314] See C. Ryan, *Transfer of Banking Supervision to the Financial Services Authority*, in M. Blair, R. Cranston, C. Ryan & M. Taylor, *Blackstone's Guide to The Bank of England Act* 1998 39 (Blackstone Press Limited 1998).

[315] M. Blair, *Introduction and Overview*, in Blair, *et al.*, *id.* at 5.

monetary system in particular; the financial system infrastructure, especially payments systems; broad oversight of the financial system as a whole; the ability to conduct what may loosely be described as official support operations; and the efficiency and effectiveness of the financial sector, with particular regard to international competitiveness. [316]

It was believed that the system that existed before the Financial Services Authority was introduced in the UK lacked transparency and adequate accountability, partly because it was so fragmented.[317] Consolidated prudential supervision of multifunctional financial groups, it was argued, provided for an efficient way of managing the risks of different financial activities (for example, traditional retail banking and securities trading)[318] while also being more publicly accountable and transparent.[319] Today, the Financial Services Authority is expected to carry out prudential financial supervision in accordance with a number of EU directives, all of which have been implemented in the UK. As Bartolini observes, "Most recently, the EU's Capital Adequacy Directive (CAD) and CAD II (implemented in the UK on January 1, 1996, and on September 30, 1998, respectively) have extended the UK supervisory picture to cover market risk and have provided scope for internal value-at-risk (VaR) models to determine risk capital."[320]

It is, however, argued that the UK regulators retain significant flexibility with respect to these directives and other international standards.[321] An example often cited is that the UK typically sets capital ratios above the Basel Accord guideline minimum of 8 percent.[322] Another example is that UK sets required capital ratios in firm-specific fashion, applying account credit and market risk factors on a consolidated basis to all financial firms within a group.[323] Furthermore, the prudential requirements applicable to authorized firms limit maximum exposure to single counter-parties or related groups.[324] The liquidity requirements emphasize two major areas: securing an institution's access to enough cash and high-quality near-cash assets to meet its obligations, and provisioning for bad and doubtful debts.[325]

---

[316] *See* Blair, *id.* at 6–7.

[317] *See* Bartolini, *The Financial Services Authority: Structure, Mandate, and Policy Issues*, in Samiei, *et al.*, *supra* n. 77, at 32.

[318] *See id.* at 31.

[319] *See id.* at 32.

[320] *See id.* at 27.

[321] *See id.*

[322] *See* for example, *id.*

[323] *See id.*

[324] *See id.* at 28.

[325] *See id.*

Experience has shown some of the shortcomings of a unified model for financial services supervision:

> Advocates of a narrow role for central banks argue that if the central bank [or whichever institution performs the role of lender of last resort (LOLR)[326]] *must* provide liquidity assistance to avert a financial crisis, then it should do so only by providing liquidity to the market at large, e.g., through open market operations, leaving to the market the task of allocating liquidity to worthy borrowers. This conduct would minimize moral hazard, both for potential beneficiaries of liquidity rescues (which would have fewer incentives to assume socially excessive risks) and for other banks (who would need to step up peer monitoring and associated market discipline). Expanding the role of a central bank to include supervisory responsibilities may also significantly raise the cost of a supervisory failure, which would damage the central bank's reputation and the credibility of its monetary policy. Furthermore, the mandates of banking supervision and of price stability are subject to a potential conflict of interest: a central bank responsible for supervision could lean toward lax monetary policy if this was perceived to avert bank failures. . . . A widely held view among advocates of an active LOLR mandate is that central banks (or whoever performs the function of LOLR) may deter the banks' tendency to assume excessive risk by keeping details of the LOLR practices "constructively" ambiguous, i.e., by retaining discretion as to whether, when, and under what conditions, emergency liquidity support will be provided.[327]

4.8   Recent Regulatory Developments in the United Kingdom

A new single Financial Services Ombudsman is now in operation in the UK. On December 1, 2001, the Financial Services Ombudsman received full powers, under the Financial Services and Markets Act 2000, to assume voluntary jurisdiction over mortgage lenders *not* authorized by the FSA and firms *not* authorized by FSA, whose activities were previously covered by membership in a former ombudsman scheme.[328] The Financial Services Ombudsman itself, under

---

[326] The IMF argues that while countries such as Germany, Japan, and—recently—Australia have separated the functions of banking supervision and lender-of-last-resort (LOLR), the U.S., Italy, and (to some extent) France have opted for a broad central bank role, combining both monetary policy/LOLR and banking supervision. For a detailed discussion, *see id.* at 36–37.

[327] *See id.* at 36 and 41.

[328] *See* The Financial Ombudsman Service, *Our Voluntary Jurisdiction,* http://www.financial-ombudsman.org.uk/vj.htm (accessed March 31, 2004).

section 227 of the 2000 Act, makes rules relating to the scope of its voluntary jurisdiction. It must be pointed out that

The Financial Services and Markets Act 2000 (FSMA) provides the statutory framework for the new UK market abuse regime, which became effective on 1 December 2001. The FSMA market abuse regime provides new powers to the Financial Services Authority (FSA) to sanction anyone who engages in "market abuse," that is misuse of information, misleading practices, and market manipulation, relating to investments traded on prescribed UK markets. It also applies to those who require or encourage others to engage in conduct that would amount to market abuse. FSMA's stated objective is to fill the "regulatory gap" by giving the FSA substantial powers to punish unregulated market participants whose market conduct falls below acceptable standards, but does not rise to the level of a criminal offence.[329]

The main statutory provisions prohibiting insider dealing in the UK can be found in Part V of the Criminal Justice Act of 1993, reinforced by Section 118 of the Financial Services and Markets Act 2000, and the proposed European Union Directive on Market Abuse.[330]

In general, the Financial Services Ombudsman receives and handles consumer complaints that do not rise to the level of a criminal offense, so that the FSA can accomplish its tasks, which include supervising wholesale markets in over-the-counter derivatives.[331] As the IMF observes:

The FSA's goal is to promote "awareness of the benefits and risks associated with different kinds of investment or other financial dealing" while safeguarding "the general principle that consumers should take responsibility for their decisions" [Financial Services and Markets Bill, Clauses 4(2)(a) and 5(2)(c)[332]]. . . . In practice, the FSA plans to protect consumers of financial services by intervening at several stages: 1) by vetting firms at

---

[329] K. Alexander, *Insider Dealing and Market Abuse: The Financial Services and Markets Act 2000*, working paper abstracted at http://ideas.repec.org/p/cbr/cbrwps/wp222.html (accessed March 31, 2004).

[330] Directive 2003/6/EC of the European Parliament and the Council of 28 January 2003 on insider dealing and market manipulation (market abuse), OJ L 96, 12.4.2003, p 16. For a further reading, *see generally* Alexander, *id.*

[331] Bartolini, *supra* n. 317, at p. 29.

[332] Bartolini argues that one of the main innovations regulatory reform has introduced into UK financial system is the separation of the functions of banking supervision (now undertaken by the Financial Services Authority) from the provision of emergency liquidity (the Bank of England will continue to be the LOLR). *See id.* at 26.

entry, to ensure that only those found to be "fit and proper" are permitted to conduct financial business; 2) by setting and enforcing prudential standards; 3) by using its powers of investigation, enforcement, and restitution against firms that fail to meet expected standards; 4) by setting a "one-stop" arrangement for resolving disputes between consumers and authorized firms—the single "Financial Services Ombudsman Scheme"; 5) by overseeing the compensation of investors when an authorized firm is unable to meet its liabilities. . . . Unsurprisingly, the approach taken by the FSA to balance consumer protection with the preservation of strong elements of *caveat emptor*—consumers must take significant responsibility for their own financial decisions—has spurred a lively debate in the UK.[333]

Under the new system that introduced the FSA, five existing compensation schemes are merged into one, the UK Financial Services and Markets Compensation Scheme (FSMC).[334] One of the notable aims of FSMC is to at least partially safeguard consumers of financial services against failure of authorized institutions to deliver on their obligations.[335] Today, the FSA has taken on new roles that were not covered by the previous regulatory regimes, among them the following:[336]

- *Mutual Societies Registration*—FSA is now responsible for the registration and public records of about 9,500 industrial and provident societies, 3,000 societies registered under the Friendly Societies legislation, 700 credit unions, and 70 building societies.
- *Unfair Terms in Consumer Contracts*—FSA has powers under the Unfair Terms in Consumer Contract Regulations 1999 to take action to deal with unfair terms in financial services consumer contracts.
- *Lloyd's Insurance Market*—FSA is responsible for regulating the Lloyd's insurance market. Large parts of the FSA Handbook (the rule book) apply to the Society of Lloyd's and the underwriting agents working in the Lloyd's market, although some provision is made for the unique nature of the market. Both the Society and underwriting agents are subject to FSA oversight, but the Society's regulatory division carries out some supervision of underwriting agents for FSA.
- *The Code of Market Conduct*—This is part of the new regime for tackling market abuse. FSA exercises powers under civil law to bridge what was a

---

[333] *See id.* at 33.

[334] *See id.* at 30.

[335] *See id.*

[336] *See* Financial Services Authority, *New Responsibilities*, http://www.fsa.gov.uk/what/new_responsibilities.html (accessed March 31, 2004).

significant gap in the ability of the UK authorities to deal with market abuse.

- *Recognized Overseas Investment Exchanges*—FSA is responsible for applications from, and supervising, recognized overseas investment exchanges (ROIEs) and recognized overseas clearing houses (ROCHs), having taken over these responsibilities from the Treasury. Current ROIEs include the Sydney Futures Exchange and NASDAQ. Recognized overseas bodies are subject to the recognition requirements laid down in the Financial Services and Markets Act 2000, which are designed to ensure that they deliver a standard of investor protection equivalent to that required of UK recognized bodies. The concept relies on the home regulators of the overseas bodies to supervise them effectively.

4.9 Conclusion

In making a case that unified financial services supervision has varied from country to country and that there is no single right way of introducing or implementing such models, this chapter has provided as case studies Latvia, the Scandinavian countries, and the UK, highlighting differences in such areas as the organization of the regulator, the objectives of regulation, and the regulatory and institutional frameworks for financial services supervision. A functional matrix organizational approach, in contrast to the sectoral approach, showed differences in how different countries have approached the introduction and implementation of unified financial services supervision. In countries where segments of the financial sector are interconnected, there is a good case for moving toward unified financial services supervision does exist.

The conclusion drawn from these country studies is that there is no strong evidence of the crystallization of best practices in the structure of unified regulators and that until there is a longer track record of experience with unified agencies, it is difficult to come to firm conclusions about the restructuring process itself, and the optimal internal structure of unified regulators.

CHAPTER 5

Conclusion

This book examined the legal aspects of the introduction of models of unified financial services supervision. It has provided an interdisciplinary exposition of the law, fleshing out practical legal and policy issues that need to be considered in drafting a law to provide for a sound framework for unified supervision of financial services. The study highlighted two fundamental questions for countries contemplating the introduction of a unified financial services regulator: Should some model of unified financial services supervision be followed? If so, how should that be done?

It is argued that countries should address these questions with reference to their own economic, institutional, and political circumstances. Reorganization of the regulatory structure may at times be ill-advised. For example, in a country that has pressing financial and economic issues, these should be dealt with first. Moreover, it is questionable whether a country facing major imminent challenges in its financial sector—such as insolvencies among major banks—should be contemplating wholesale reorganization of the regulatory function, which might deflect attention away from the problems at hand. In other countries, as this study points out, where the various segments of the financial sector (insurance, securities, pensions, and banking) have very little connection with each other, maintaining the status quo would be more appropriate, at least in the short term. Some countries may not even have enough financial resources and well-trained human capital to implement unified financial services supervision.

Although there is not much evidence of the existence of broadly accepted standards of best practices in the structuring of unified financial services regulators, there is some evidence of common threads that could guide policy makers and law reform institutions in the design of a sound legal framework for the unified supervision of financial services.[337] In particular, the legal and regulatory framework should be designed so as to protect investors and consumers and to help build investor confidence in the market. Also, the design should aim at establishing a fair, transparent, and efficient market that reduces systemic risk. The law should protect financial services businesses from malpractices of some consumers while promoting consumer confidence in the financial system. Regulators and supervisors should be afforded judicial immunity against lawsuits

---

[337] *See generally, International Developments Parts I* and *II, supra* n. 1.

for actions or omissions done in good faith and in the course of business. From an economic standpoint, the framework should be able to provide incentives to redress the information imbalance that sometimes exists between consumers and financial services businesses in favor of consumers. This goal can be achieved by imposing minimum standards of business conduct for financial services businesses.

It is possible for a country to have more than one level of regulation guiding the supervision of financial services. Canada, for example, has two main tiers. While the Office of the Superintendent of Financial Institutions (OSFI) is the primary regulator of federally chartered financial institutions, such as some insurance companies, pension funds, trusts, and loans companies,[338] the regulation of securities on Canadian stock exchanges is left to provincial agencies. This bicameral structure aligns itself with the Canadian Constitution, which requires all banks, federally incorporated insurance companies, pension funds, trusts, and loan companies to be licensed and regulated at the federal level. These are the primary institutions OSFI regulates. Though by law, all banks must be incorporated and regulated at the federal level,[339] some insurance companies, trusts, and loan companies are provincially chartered and thus are licensed and regulated by the provinces.[340] Securities firms are incorporated at the provincial level and are, like other financial institutions chartered at the provincial level, subject to the laws and licensing requirements of the province where incorporation and licensing has taken place.

The cardinal point here is that in Canada unified financial services supervision applies principally to institutions regulated at the federal level, not to those regulated at the provincial level. This model is unique to Canada, demonstrating that every country has country-specific conditions that necessitate a particular way of introducing and implementing unified financial services supervision.

---

[338] By virtue of the Canadian Constitution—The Constitution Act, 1867, 30 & 31 Victoria, c. 3. (U.K.)—the mission of OSFI is to safeguard policy holders, depositors, and pension plan members from undue loss. OSFI supervises and regulates all banks and all federally incorporated or registered trust and loan companies, insurance companies, cooperative credit associations, fraternal benefit societies, and pension plans. As explained on the OSFI website (http://www.osfi-bsif.gc.ca/eng/default.asp?ref=home, accessed April 4, 2004): "OSFI is committed to providing professional, high-quality and cost-effective service. This is achieved by advancing and administering a regulatory framework that contributes to public confidence in the financial services industry. At the same time, OSFI ensures the regulatory system does not preclude institutions from competing effectively."

[339] *See generally* the British–North American Act 1867 (the Canadian Constitution).

[340] In Canada, a notable feature of provincial-level licensing is that a financial institution chartered at the provincial level must be licensed separately in every province where it decides to conduct financial services business, whereas other financial institutions licensed and regulated at the federal level are under no obligation to seek provincial licensing if they decide to undertake financial services business in any province.

There have been efforts in the past to set up a Canadian nationwide securities regulator, akin to the U.S. Securities and Exchange Commission, but the results have been minimal, mainly because the provinces are unwilling to give up their regulatory powers. Thus, although some commentators might want to argue that Canada could benefit from a model of supervisory unification like that of the UK, the historical and constitutional background to Canada's regulatory framework poses some interesting challenges. To overcome some of those posed by the Canadian Constitution to prospects for full unification of the supervisory functions in Canada, the Hockin-Kwinter Accord[341] defines special procedures for how federal regulators can gain access to information on securities firms that are owned by banks.

In Canada, a bank that in addition to its normal banking business provides investment advice or deals in securities must also obtain authorization from the competent provincial securities regulator. Similarly, collective investment schemes, such as mutual funds or unit trusts, that are involved in securities trade and investment require provincial authorization. Thus, the structure of securities regulation in Canada that has evolved historically incorporates both federal and provincial laws.

Depending on country-specific conditions and the objectives of introducing a unified regulator, this book argues that the regulatory framework in any country can combine any instruments, such as primary and secondary legislation, and principles, rules, codes, or guidance or policy directives issued by the regulator. Some countries have fewer levels of regulation, others have more. How the regulatory framework is structured depends on a host of factors, some of which are entirely political and ideological.

Overall, it is important to ensure that a unified regulator is clothed with the statutory and regulatory powers that enable it to carry out its functions responsibly and efficiently. Most unified regulators have been given statutory powers to authorize a business to conduct regulated activities and to supervise regulated businesses. In a number of cases, unified regulators have powers to inspect, investigate, and enforce compliance with legal requirements, either by imposing license requirements or withdrawing authorization to do business. In addition, if a unified regulator is to function efficiently, it must be able to tap into the information resources of other regulators, by sharing relevant information with them. These are some of the notable factors that must be considered in drafting a good law or designing a sound regulatory framework for unified financial services supervision.

Further, the design of an efficient framework for unified financial services supervision should factor in a structure for the regulator that is based on sound

---

[341] *See generally, International Developments Parts I* and *II, supra* n. 1.

principles of corporate governance. The regulatory framework should strike a balance between the independence and the accountability of the regulator, assigning adequate apolitical powers to appoint and dismiss the Chief Executive Officer of the regulator, identifying minimum qualifications for appointment to that position, spelling out the transparency with which decisions of the regulatory body should be made, promoting client confidentiality, regulating timely and adequate disclosure of information, and penalizing market abuses and misconducts.

Evidence presented in chapter 3 showed that the process of and the obstacles encountered in structuring a unified regulator have differed from country to country, thus undermining any case for best practices of unified financial services supervision. It may be concluded that any decision to set up a unified regulator should be preceded by well-prepared feasibility studies that, for example, identify evidence of strong interconnectedness among the segments of the financial sector, threats of systemic risk and contagion, the emergence of universal banking, increases in product innovation in the financial market, increases in the number of group companies operating in it, the internationalization of businesses in the financial sector, and other features already examined above.

It is of paramount importance that the regulatory framework address the sharing of information between a host regulator and foreign regulators as needed, or between a unified regulator and other stakeholders in the financial sector, such as the central bank, a deposit insurance agency, the Ministry of Finance, the tax authority, and the registrar of companies. In many countries, including the United Kingdom, Hungary, and Zambia, such efforts are being addressed through a memorandum of understanding that brings various stakeholders to the table. It is advisable that countries contemplating the introduction of a unified regulator consider a memorandum-of-understanding strategy to encourage information sharing.

APPENDIX **1**

The Estonian Financial Supervisory Authority Act, 2001*

Chapter 1

General Provisions

§ 1. Scope of application of Act
This Act determines the objective of state financial supervision and the legal status, the bases for the activities and the bases and procedure for the financing of the Financial Supervisory Authority.

§ 2. State financial supervision
(1) For the purposes of this Act, state financial supervision (hereinafter financial supervision) is the supervision of subjects of state financial supervision (hereinafter subjects of financial supervision) and of the activities provided for in this Act, the Credit Institutions Act (RT[1] I 1999, 23, 349; 2000, 35, 222; 40, 250), the Insurance Activities Act (RT I 2000, 53, 343; 2001, 43, 238), the Insurance Act (RT 1992, 48, 601; RT I 1995, 26–28, 355; 1996, 23, 455; 40, 773; 1998, 61, 979; 1999, 10, 155; 27, 389; 2000, 53, 343; 2001, 43, 238), the Investment Funds Act (RT I 1997, 34, 535; 1998, 61, 979; 2000, 10, 55; 57, 373), the Pension Funds Act (RT I 1998, 61, 979), the Securities Market Act (RT I 1993, 35, 543; 1995, 22, 328; 1996, 26, 528; 1997, 34, 535; 1998, 61, 979; 2000, 10, 55), the Estonian Central Register of Securities Act (RT I 2000, 57, 373), and legislation established on the basis thereof.

(2) For the purposes of this Act, a subject of financial supervision is a person to whom the right to operate in the corresponding field of activity has been granted by a competent authority on the basis of an Act specified in subsection (1) of this section.

§ 3. Objective of financial supervision
Financial supervision is conducted in order to enhance the stability, reliability, transparency and efficiency of the financial sector, to reduce systemic risks and

---

* Unofficial translation, available at <http://www.legaltext.ee/text/en/X50008K4.htm>.
[1] RT = Riigi Teataja = the State Gazette

93

to promote prevention of the abuse of the financial sector for criminal purposes, with a view to protecting the interests of clients and investors by safeguarding their financial resources, and thereby supporting the stability of the Estonian monetary system.

§ 4. Financial Supervisory Authority

(1) The Financial Supervisory Authority (hereinafter the Supervisory Authority) is an agency with autonomous competence and a separate budget, which operates at the Bank of Estonia and the directing bodies of which act and submit reports pursuant to the procedure provided for in this Act.

(2) The Supervisory Authority conducts financial supervision in the name of the state.

(3) The Supervisory Authority is independent in the conduct of financial supervision.

§ 5. Principles of activities of Supervisory Authority

The Supervisory Authority shall operate pursuant to legislation and the internationally recognized principles relating to financial supervision and shall act openly and transparently and apply the principles of sound administration. The Supervisory Authority shall use the assets at its disposal prudently.

§ 6. Functions and rights of Supervisory Authority

(1) The functions of the Supervisory Authority in fulfilling the objectives of financial supervision are to:

1) analyse and monitor constantly the compliance of subjects of financial supervision with the requirements for financial soundness and own funds, and other obligations prescribed by the Bank of Estonia Act (RT I 1993, 28, 498; 30, correction notice; 1994, 30, 463; 1998, 64/65, 1006; 1999, 16, 271), the Acts specified in subsection 2 (1) of this Act, and legislation established on the basis thereof;

2) guide and direct subjects of financial supervision in order to ensure sound and prudent management;

3) apply measures prescribed by legislation to protect the interests of clients and investors;

4) apply administrative coercion on the bases, to the extent and pursuant to the procedure prescribed by Acts;

5) make proposals for the establishment and amendment of Acts and other legislation concerning the financial sector and related supervision, and participate in the drafting of such Acts and legislation;

6) co-operate with international financial supervision organizations and foreign financial supervision authorities and other competent foreign authorities and persons;

7) perform the functions arising from the Deposit Guarantee Fund Act (RT I 1998, 40, 612) and the Money Laundering Prevention Act (RT I 1998, 110, 1811; 2000, 84, 533);

8) perform other functions arising from law which are necessary to fulfill the objectives of financial supervision.

(2) In the performance of its functions, the Supervisory Authority has all the rights provided for in this Act, the Acts specified in subsection 2 (1) of this Act and legislation established on the basis thereof.

Chapter 2

Management of Financial Supervisory Authority

Division 1

Supervisory Board

§ 7. Competence of supervisory board

(1) The activities of the Supervisory Authority shall be planned and the management thereof shall be monitored by the supervisory board of the Supervisory Authority (hereinafter the supervisory board).

(2) The supervisory board shall:

1) approve the operating strategy of the Supervisory Authority at the proposal of the management board of the Supervisory Authority (hereinafter the management board);

2) approve, on the proposal of the management board, the budget of the Supervisory Authority and, in the case specified in § 45 of this Act, the supplementary budget, and make a proposal to the Minister of Finance concerning the rate of the share of the supervision fee calculated on the basis of assets for the following budgetary year;

3) approve, on the proposal of the management board, the bases for developing the structure of the Supervisory Authority and for the payment of remuneration;

4) appoint the members of the management board and elect the chairman of the management board from among the members;

5) remove members of the management board;

6) decide on entry into, amendment of and termination of contracts of service with the chairman and members of the management board;

7) approve the size of the remuneration and additional sums payable and the social guarantees applicable to the chairman and members of the management board;

8) decide on the filing of a claim against the chairman or a member of the management board concerning compensation for damage caused by him or her to the state through violation of a legal act or his or her obligations;

9) approve the annual report of the Supervisory Authority submitted by the management board;

10) approve the rules for the activities of the supervisory board.

§ 8. Members of supervisory board

(1) The supervisory board shall consist of six members, two of whom are members by virtue of office and four of whom are appointed members.

(2) The Minister of Finance and the President of the Bank of Estonia are members of the supervisory board by virtue of office.

(3) One-half of the appointed members of the supervisory board shall be appointed and removed by the Government of the Republic on the proposal of the Minister of Finance and one-half by the Board of the Bank of Estonia on the proposal of the President of the Bank of Estonia.

§ 9. Requirements for members of supervisory board

(1) Appointed members of the supervisory board shall be Estonian citizens with active legal capacity, an academic degree recognized by the state or education corresponding to such level, an impeccable professional and business reputation, and the experience necessary to manage an agency in the financial or public sector.

(2) The following shall not be appointed as members of the supervisory board:

1) persons under preliminary investigation for or accused of a criminal offence for which the law prescribes imprisonment or persons with a criminal record for criminal official misconduct or any other intentionally committed criminal offence;

2) persons whose previous unlawful act or omission has resulted in the bankruptcy, compulsory dissolution or revocation of the activity licence of a company;

3) bankrupts or persons who are subject to a prohibition on business or from whom the right to engage in economic activity has been taken away pursuant to law.

(3) The provisions of subsections 32 (1) and (2) of this Act concerning the avoidance of conflicts of interests and the provisions of § 34 of this Act concerning the duty to maintain confidentiality apply to members of the supervisory board.

§ 10. Term of authority of members of supervisory board

(1) The authority of a member of the supervisory board specified in subsection 8 (2) of this Act shall expire upon the expiry of his or her authority in the office by virtue of which he or she belongs to the supervisory board.

(2) The term of the authority of appointed members of the supervisory board shall be three years as of their appointment.

(3) Upon expiry of the term of the authority of an appointed member, he or she shall perform his or her duties until the appointment of a new member.

(4) Upon expiry of the term of the authority or the removal or death of an appointed member of the supervisory board, the person who initially appointed the member shall appoint a new member of the supervisory board within a reasonable period of time.

§ 11. Removal of member of supervisory board

(1) An appointed member of the supervisory board is removed before the expiry of his or her term of authority within three months after receipt of a corresponding written application from the member.

(2) An appointed member of the supervisory board shall be immediately removed before the expiry of his or her term of authority if:

1) a judgment of conviction made against him or her in a criminal matter enters into force;

2) he or she violates the provisions of subsection 32 (1) or (2) or § 34 of this Act;

3) a bankruptcy order enters into force or a prohibition on business is applied with regard to him or her or the right to engage in economic activity is taken away from him or her pursuant to law;

4) he or she does not comply with the requirements established by this Act for appointed members or submits false information concerning compliance with such requirements.

(3) An appointed member of the supervisory board may be removed before the expiry of his or her term of authority if he or she suffers from an illness lasting for more than four months or if there is any other good reason due to which he or she is unable to perform his or her duties.

§ 12. Chairman of supervisory board

(1) The Minister of Finance shall be the chairman of the supervisory board.

(2) The chairman of the supervisory board shall organise the activities and administration of the supervisory board, call and chair the meetings of the supervisory board, organise the taking of minutes at the meetings and disclosure of the resolutions of the supervisory board and enter into, amend, suspend and terminate contracts of service with the chairman and members of the management board on the basis of a resolution of the supervisory board.

(3) In the absence of the chairman of the supervisory board, the duties of the chairman shall be performed by the eldest member of the supervisory board present at the meeting.

§ 13. Calling meetings of supervisory board

(1) Regular meetings of the supervisory board shall be held at least once every three months.

(2) Extraordinary meetings of the supervisory board shall be called on the initiative of the chairman of the supervisory board at the request of at least two members of the supervisory board or the chairman of the management board. The request shall set out the matters to be decided and a proposal concerning the time of the meeting.

(3) A notice concerning an ordinary meeting of the supervisory board shall be sent to the members of the supervisory board at least ten days before the date of the meeting. Members of the supervisory board shall be notified of an extraordinary meeting of the supervisory board at least one working day in advance.

(4) A notice calling a meeting of the supervisory board shall set out the time and place of the meeting and the agenda together with the names of the persons presenting reports.

§ 14. Organisation of activities of supervisory board

(1) Members of the supervisory board shall personally participate in the activities of the supervisory board.

(2) Meetings of the supervisory board shall be closed unless the supervisory board decides otherwise.

(3) Members of the management board have the right to participate in the meetings of the supervisory board unless the chairman of the supervisory board decides otherwise.

(4) Issues relating to meetings of the supervisory board shall be provided for in the rules for the activities of the supervisory board, including:

    1) the procedure for the election of the chairman of the management board;

    2) the procedure for giving notice of meetings of the supervisory board;

    3) the procedure for communicating documents concerning the agenda of a meeting to the members of the supervisory board;

4) the information to be recorded in the minutes of a meeting, including the content of the resolutions of the supervisory board and issues relating to the recording of voting results;

5) the procedure for adoption of resolutions of the supervisory board without calling a meeting, the information to be entered in records of votes and the procedure for preservation of draft resolutions and the positions and dissenting opinions of the members of the supervisory board.

(5) Members of the supervisory board shall receive monthly remuneration in the amount of twice the minimum monthly wage.

(6) The technical administration of the activities of the supervisory board shall be ensured by the management board.

§ 15. Resolutions of supervisory board

(1) Each member of the supervisory board has one vote. Unless otherwise provided by this Act, members of the supervisory board do not have the right to abstain from voting or to remain undecided.

(2) A resolution of the supervisory board is adopted if at least four members of the supervisory board vote in favor. In matters specified in clause 7 (2) 10) of this Act, a resolution of the supervisory board is adopted if all members of the supervisory board vote in favor.

(3) A member of the supervisory board shall give notice to the supervisory board if he or she is directly or indirectly personally interested in a resolution to be debated. A member of the supervisory board is required to give notice if his or her child, parent, sister, brother, spouse or cohabitee, or a parent, child, brother or sister of his or her spouse or cohabitee is:

1) a member of the management board or a person to be appointed as a member of the management board, before voting on issues provided for in clauses 7 (2) 4)–8) of this Act;

2) a person required to pay the supervision fee specified in subsections 36 (1)–(3) of this Act or a shareholder with a qualifying holding in such person or a person who exercises dominant influence on the management thereof in any other manner or is a member of its management body, before voting on issues provided for in clause 7 (2) 2) of this Act.

(4) If circumstances specified in subsection (3) of this section become evident, the member of the supervisory board shall abstain from voting unless all other members of the supervisory board who participate in the vote agree to his or her voting.

(5) A member of the supervisory board who votes against a resolution of the supervisory board has the right to submit his or her dissenting opinion.

§ 16. Minutes of meetings of supervisory board

(1) Minutes shall be taken of meetings of the supervisory board.

(2) The chairman of the supervisory board and the secretary shall sign the minutes.

(3) Written dissenting opinions submitted by members of the supervisory board shall be annexed to the minutes. A notation shall be made in the minutes concerning the annexing of a dissenting opinion, and the member of the supervisory board who submitted the opinion shall confirm the notation with his or her signature.

(4) Minutes of meetings of the supervisory board shall be preserved in the Supervisory Authority indefinitely. The management board shall organise storage of the minutes and annexes thereto and shall be responsible for their preservation.

§ 17. Adoption of resolutions without calling meeting

(1) The supervisory board has the right to adopt resolutions without calling a meeting of the supervisory board if all members of the supervisory board consent thereto and hold a certificate for giving digital signatures issued pursuant to the Digital Signatures Act (RT I 2000, 26, 150; 92, 597).

(2) The supervisory board does not have the right to adopt resolutions on issues specified in clauses 7 (2) 1), 4) or 10) of this Act without calling a meeting of the supervisory board.

(3) Upon adoption of a resolution of the supervisory board in the manner provided for in subsection (1) of this section, all proposals, positions and decisions shall be certified by digital signatures.

(4) The chairman of the supervisory board shall send a draft resolution to all members of the supervisory board and specify the term by which the members of the supervisory board must present their positions. If a member of the supervisory board fails to present his or her position within the specified term, he or she is deemed to have voted against the resolution.

(5) The provisions of § 15 of this Act apply to the adoption of resolutions.

(6) Minutes shall be taken of voting results and shall be sent immediately to all members of the supervisory board and to the management board.

Division 2
Management Board

§ 18. Competence of management board

(1) The management board shall manage and organise the activities of the Supervisory Authority. The management board is competent to adopt all resolutions relating to the performance of the obligations of the Supervisory Authority and

to perform all obligations and exercise all rights which pursuant to this Act are not in the competence of the supervisory board, the chairman of the supervisory board or the chairman of the management board. The management board shall execute the resolutions made by the supervisory board pursuant to subsection 7 (2) of this Act.

(2) In issues relating to the conduct of financial supervision on the bases provided for in the Acts specified in subsection 2 (1) of this Act, the management board shall decide on:

1) the issue and revocation of activity licenses and other issues relating to activity licenses;

2) the grant of consent, permission or concordance;

3) issues relating to performance of the registration obligation and entering items in lists;

4) the issue of precepts;

5) the application of administrative coercive measures;

6) the imposition of administrative penalties;

7) the ordering of special audits or expert assessments;

8) the establishment of a moratorium or a special regime and the performance of related acts;

9) the filing of bankruptcy petitions and the performance of other acts relating to bankruptcy or liquidation proceedings.

(3) In issues relating to the management and organisation of activities, the management board shall:

1) submit the strategy of the Supervisory Authority to the supervisory board for approval;

2) submit the draft budget of the Supervisory Authority to the supervisory board for approval together with a proposal concerning the rate of the share of the supervision fee calculated on the basis of assets, payable on the basis of this Act for the following budgetary year;

3) submit the draft supplementary budget to the supervisory board for approval in the case provided for in § 45 of this Act;

4) decide, pursuant to and to the extent of the budget approved by the supervisory board, on the acquisition and transfer of immovables and of movables to be entered in a register;

5) submit proposals to the supervisory board concerning development of the structure of the Supervisory Authority and the bases for payment of remuneration;

6) approve the structure and staff of the Supervisory Authority pursuant to the bases approved by the supervisory board;

7) approve the accounting policies and procedures of the Supervisory Authority;

8) submit the report provided for in subsection 49 (1) of this Act to the supervisory board for their information;

9) approve the procedure for conducting internal audits of the Supervisory Authority;

10) if necessary, involve experts in the conduct of financial supervision;

11) form work groups and committees for the performance of the functions of the Supervisory Authority;

12) decide on entry into co-operation agreements specified in § 50 of this Act;

13) decide on entry into co-operation agreements with foreign financial supervision authorities and other competent foreign bodies or persons;

14) submit an overview of the activities of the Supervisory Authority and an income and expense statement to the supervisory board once per quarter;

15) submit the annual report of the Supervisory Authority to the supervisory board for approval;

16) approve the rules for the activities of the management board;

17) decide on other issues relating to the organisation of the regular activities of the Supervisory Authority if such decision is requested by at least two members of the management board.

§ 19. Members of management board

(1) The management board shall consist of five members.

(2) The members of the management board shall be appointed and removed by the supervisory board.

§ 20. Requirements for members of management board

(1) Members of the management board must be Estonian citizens with active legal capacity and an academic degree recognized by the state or education corresponding to such level, the expertise necessary to manage the Supervisory Authority, professional suitability, an impeccable professional and business reputation and a total of at least five years' work experience in the fields of finance, law, auditing or information technology or in public service in a position relating to such fields.

(2) The following shall not be appointed as members of the management board:

1) members of the supervisory board;

2) members of the Board of the Bank of Estonia or the Executive Management of the Bank of Estonia;

3) auditors of the Bank of Estonia;

4) persons under preliminary investigation for or accused of a criminal offence for which the law prescribes imprisonment or persons with a criminal record for criminal official misconduct or any other intentionally committed criminal offence;

5) persons whose previous unlawful act or omission has resulted in the bankruptcy, compulsory dissolution or revocation of the activity licence of a company;

6) bankrupts or persons who are subject to a prohibition on business or from whom the right to engage in economic activity has been taken away pursuant to law.

(3) Members of the management board shall not be public servants nor work for any other employer or in a structural unit or independent division of the Bank of Estonia.

(4) The provisions of § 31, subsections 32 (1) and (2) and § 34 of this Act apply to members of the management board.

(5) Before a person is appointed as a member of the management board, he or she shall submit the information specified in subsection 32 (3) of this Act to the supervisory board in writing and confirmation that no circumstances exist which according to this Act would preclude his or her appointment as a member of the management board. The member of the management board shall notify the supervisory board immediately of any changes in the information submitted.

§ 21. Term of authority of members of management board

(1) The term of the authority of members of the management board shall be three years.

(2) The term of the authority of the member of the management board who is the chairman of the management board shall be four years.

(3) The authority of a member of the management board shall commence as of the date specified in the resolution concerning his or her appointment.

(4) The chairman of the supervisory board shall enter into contracts of service with the chairman and the members of the management board for the term of their authority and the contracts shall specify the rights and duties of the members of the management board and the remuneration for the performance of the duties of chairman or members of the management board.

§ 22. Removal of member of management board

(1) A member of the management board is removed before the expiry of his or her term of authority not later than within three months after receipt of a corresponding written application from the member.

(2) A member of the management board shall be immediately removed before the expiry of his or her term of authority if:

1) a judgment of conviction made against him or her in a criminal matter enters into force;

2) he or she violates the provisions of subsection 32 (1) or (2) or § 34 of this Act;

3) a bankruptcy order enters into force or a prohibition on business is applied with regard to him or her or the right to engage in economic activity is taken away from him or her pursuant to law;

4) he or she does not comply with the requirements established by this Act for members of the management board or submits false information concerning compliance with such requirements.

(3) A member of the management board may be removed before the expiry of his or her term of authority if he or she suffers from an illness lasting for more than four months or if there is any other good reason due to which he or she is unable to perform his or her duties.

(4) Upon expiry of the term of the authority or the removal or death of a member of the management board, the supervisory board shall appoint a new member of the management board within a reasonable period of time.

§ 23. Chairman of management board

(1) The supervisory board shall elect the chairman of the management board from among the members of the management board pursuant to the procedure provided for in the rules for the activities of the supervisory board. In the absence of the chairman of the management board, the duties of the chairman shall be performed by the eldest member of the management board unless otherwise ordered by a directive of the chairman of the management board.

(2) The chairman of the management board shall:

1) organise the activities of the management board;

2) call and chair the meetings of the management board and organise the taking of minutes at the meetings;

3) organise the administration of the Supervisory Authority and the disclosure of the activities of the Supervisory Authority;

4) organise the accounting of the Supervisory Authority;

5) decide on the making of expenditure necessary for the activities of the Supervisory Authority according to and to the extent of the budget approved by the supervisory board;

6) enter into, amend, suspend and terminate employment contracts with employees.

(3) The chairman of the management board shall represent the Supervisory Authority in court and in relations with other state agencies, the Bank of Estonia, other persons, international organizations for financial supervision, foreign financial supervision authorities and other competent foreign authorities, organizations and persons.

(4) On the basis of a resolution of the management board, the chairman of the management board shall issue authorization documents to other members of the management board, employees and third parties who represent the Supervisory Authority.

§ 24. Calling meetings of management board
(1) Meetings of the management board shall be held when necessary but not less frequently than once a month.

(2) Meetings of the management board shall be called by the chairman of the management board on his or her own initiative or on the proposal of a member of the management board.

§ 25. Organisation of meetings of management board
(1) Meetings of the management board shall be closed unless the chairman of the management board decides otherwise.

(2) Issues relating to meetings of the management board shall be provided for in the rules for the activities of the management board, including:

1) the procedure for giving notice of meetings of the management board;

2) the procedure for communicating documents concerning the agenda of a meeting to the members of the management board;

3) the information to be recorded in the minutes of a meeting, including the content of the resolutions of the management board and issues relating to the recording of voting results;

4) the procedure for the adoption of resolutions of the management board without calling a meeting, the information to be recorded in records of votes and the procedure for preservation of draft resolutions and the positions and dissenting opinions of the members of the management board.

§ 26. Resolutions of management board

(1) Each member of the management board has one vote. Members of the management board do not have the right to abstain from voting or to remain undecided.

(2) A resolution of the management board is adopted if at least three members of the management board vote in favor.

(3) A member of the management board who votes against a resolution of the management board has the right to submit his or her dissenting opinion.

(4) A member of the management board shall give notice to the management board if his or her child, parent, sister, brother, spouse or cohabitee, or a child, parent, sister or brother of his or her spouse or cohabitee is a member of the management body, procurator, other representative, head of the internal audit unit, chairman of the audit committee or auditor of or shareholder with a qualifying holding in a relevant subject of financial supervision, or a person exercising dominant influence over the management of such company in any other manner or a director or representative of an Estonian branch of a foreign company.

(5) Members of the management board specified in subsection (4) of this section may participate in voting if all other members of the management board participating in the vote are in favor thereof.

§ 27. Minutes of meetings of management board

(1) Minutes shall be taken of meetings of the management board.

(2) Written dissenting opinions submitted by members of the management board shall be annexed to the minutes. A notation shall be made in the minutes concerning the annexing of a dissenting opinion, and the member of the management board who submitted the opinion shall confirm the notation with his or her signature.

(3) The chairman of the management board and the secretary shall sign the minutes.

(4) Minutes of meetings of the management board shall be preserved in the Supervisory Authority indefinitely.

§ 28. Adoption of resolutions without calling meeting

(1) The management board has the right to adopt resolutions without calling a meeting of the management board if all members of the management board consent thereto and hold a certificate for giving digital signatures issued pursuant to the Digital Signatures Act.

(2) Upon adoption of a resolution of the management board in the manner provided for in subsection (1) of this section, all proposals, positions and decisions shall be certified by digital signatures.

(3) The chairman of the management board shall send a draft resolution to all members of the management board and specify the term by which the members of the management board must present their positions. If a member of the management board fails to present his or her position within the specified term, he or she is deemed to have voted against the resolution.

(4) The provisions of § 26 of this Act apply to the adoption of resolutions.

(5) Minutes shall be taken of voting results and shall be sent immediately to all members of the management board.

§ 29. Liability of members of management board
(1) Members of the management board shall be solidarily liable for any damage wrongfully caused by their unlawful behavior.

(2) A member of the management board is required to compensate the state for any damage caused by violation of his or her duties intentionally or through gross negligence. Compensation claimed for damage caused through gross negligence shall not exceed six times the monthly remuneration paid to the member of the management board.

(3) A member of the management board shall be released from liability if, upon adoption of a resolution which is in conflict with the law, he or she holds a position which is in accordance with the law and submits a corresponding dissenting opinion which is annexed to the minutes.

(4) The limitation period for a claim against a member of the management board shall be three years as of the commission of the violation.

Chapter 3

Requirements for Employees

§ 30. Employees of Supervisory Authority
(1) Employees of the Supervisory Authority (hereinafter employees) and members of the management board of the Supervisory Authority shall be subject to the Republic of Estonia Employment Contracts Act (RT 1992, 15/16, 241; 1993, 10, 150; RT I 1993, 26, 441; 1995, 14, 170; 16, 228; 1996, 3, 57; 40, 773; 45, 850; 49, 953; 1997, 5/6, 32; 1998, 111, 1829; 1999, 16, 276; 60, 616; 2000, 25, 144; 51, 327; 57, 370; 102, 669; 2001, 17, 78; 42, 233) and other labor laws unless otherwise provided by this Act.

(2) Persons may be employed by the Supervisory Authority if they have the necessary education, sufficient experience and professional qualifications to perform their duties and an impeccable professional and business reputation.

(3) The following shall not be employed:

1) persons under preliminary investigation for or accused of a criminal offence or persons with a criminal record for criminal official misconduct;

2) persons whose previous unlawful act or omission has resulted in the bankruptcy, compulsory dissolution or revocation of the activity licence of a company;

3) bankrupts or persons who are subject to a prohibition on business or from whom the right to work in a particular position or operate in a particular area of activity has been taken away pursuant to law.

(4) Before an employment contract is entered into with a person applying for employment, he or she is required to submit to the management board a written overview of his or her education, qualifications, in-service training, professional experience and business activities, the information specified in subsection 32 (3) of this Act, and confirmation that no circumstances exist which according to this Act would preclude his or her right to be an employee.

(5) Upon entry into an employment contract, a probationary period of up to six months may be applied.

(6) An employment contract may be entered into with an employee for an unspecified term or for a term of up to five years.

§ 31. Duties of employees

(1) An employee is required to perform his or her duties in good faith, adhere to good practice and act with the conscientiousness necessary for the exercise of public authority, with the prudence and competence expected of him or her and according to the requirements for his or her position.

(2) An employee shall refrain from acts which are or may be detrimental to the objectives, functions or reputation of the Supervisory Authority.

§ 32. Avoiding conflicts of interest

(1) An employee shall not be a shareholder with a qualifying holding in a subject of financial supervision, a person who exercises dominant influence over the management of such subject in any other manner or a member of the management body or a procurator thereof, a person who holds the right of representation on any other basis, or the auditor, head of the internal audit unit or chairman of the audit committee thereof, or a director or representative of an Estonian branch of a foreign company.

(2) An employee shall not enter into agreements with a subject of financial supervision or persons specified in subsection (1) of this section according to which the employee is required to provide investment or consulting services.

(3) Before an employment contract is entered into with a person applying for employment with the Supervisory Authority, he or she shall, in the format

established by the Minister of Finance, submit information to the management board concerning his or her proprietary obligations and those of his or her spouse or cohabitee, children and parents to subjects of financial supervision, and information concerning the securities owned by the abovementioned persons. The employee shall immediately notify the management board of any relevant changes in the information submitted.

§ 33. Removal

(1) An employee shall not participate in supervision proceedings or in the preparation of a resolution of the management board if he or she is directly or indirectly personally interested in the matter.

(2) An employee is required to notify the chairman of the management board immediately if the circumstances specified in subsection (1) of this section exist or if his or her child, parent, sister, brother, spouse or cohabitee, or a child, parent, sister or brother of his or her spouse or cohabitee is a member of the management body, procurator, other representative, head of the internal audit unit, chairman of the audit committee or auditor of or shareholder with a qualifying holding in a relevant subject of financial supervision, or a person exercising dominant influence over the management of such company in any other manner or a director or representative of an Estonian branch of a foreign company.

(3) If the chairman of the management board has reasonable doubt about the impartiality of an employee, the chairman has the right to remove the employee from supervision proceedings or the preparation of a resolution of the management board.

§ 34. Duty to maintain confidentiality

(1) Unless otherwise provided by this Act, employees of the Supervisory Authority and the auditors, experts and other persons brought in by the Supervisory Authority to participate in the conduct of financial supervision are required to maintain indefinitely the confidentiality of any confidential information which they may receive while performing their duties in the Supervisory Authority.

(2) Persons specified in subsection (1) of this section shall not use any confidential information which they may receive while performing their duties for their private interests.

Chapter 4

Financing

§ 35. Sources of financing

(1) The expenses of the Supervisory Authority shall be covered from the compulsory payments made by the subjects of financial supervision pursuant to the

provisions of this Act (hereinafter the supervision fee) and, in the case provided for in § 45 of this Act, from the funds prescribed in the budget of the Bank of Estonia and appropriations prescribed in the state budget.

(2) The supervision fee consists of the capital share and the share calculated on the basis of assets.

§ 36. Financing obligation

(1) The organisation specified in subsection 75 (1) of the Insurance Activities Act (hereinafter Lloyd's), investment firms, insurers, insurance brokers, credit institutions and management companies shall pay a supervision fee in the amount of the capital share and the share calculated on the basis of assets.

(2) The registrar of the Estonian Central Register of Securities, operators of clearing and settlement systems and operators of regulated securities markets shall pay a supervision fee only in the amount of the capital share.

(3) Unless otherwise provided by this Act, an Estonian branch of a foreign company, operating in the area of activity of an investment firm, insurer, insurance broker, credit institution or management company, shall pay a supervision fee only in the amount of the share calculated on the basis of assets.

(4) The financing obligation provided for in subsections (1)–(3) of this section (hereinafter the financing obligation) of the persons specified in those subsections or of an Estonian branch of a foreign company operating in the corresponding area of activity arises as of the entry of the corresponding area of activity of the person or branch in the commercial register. The financing obligation of an insurance broker arises as of the entry of the insurance broker in the list of insurance intermediaries.

(5) The financing obligation of a person specified in subsections (1)–(3) of this section or an Estonian branch of a foreign company expires upon the expiry of the corresponding right to operate and the financing obligation of an insurance broker expires upon the deletion of the broker from the list of insurance intermediaries.

(6) Upon the expiry of a financing obligation, the supervision fee shall not be refunded.

§ 37. Rate of supervision fee

(1) The capital share of the supervision fee is an amount equal to one per cent of:

  1) the minimum amount of the net own funds required pursuant to legislation in the case of a credit institution;

  2) the highest amount of minimum own funds required pursuant to legislation in order to engage in the class of insurance specified in the activity licence, in the case of an insurer;

3) the highest amount of minimum own funds required pursuant to legislation in the case of the Estonian Central Register of Securities or an operator of a clearing and settlement system;

4) the highest amount of minimum share capital required pursuant to legislation in order to operate in the area of activity specified in the activity licence, in the case of an investment firm, operator of a regulated securities market or a management company;

5) the minimum amount of share capital required pursuant to legislation in the case of an insurance broker;

6) the amount provided for in clause 75 (6) 3) of the Insurance Activities Act in the case of Lloyd's.

(2) The share of the supervision fee calculated on the basis of assets is an amount equal to:

1) in the case of a credit institution or an Estonian branch of a foreign company operating as a credit institution, 0.01 to 0.05 per cent of the assets of the credit institution or the corresponding Estonian branch;

2) in the case of an investment firm or an Estonian branch of a foreign company operating as an investment firm, 0.4 to 0.75 per cent of the assets of the investment firm or the corresponding Estonian branch;

3) in the case of a management company or an Estonian branch of a foreign company operating as a management company, 0.05 to 0.25 per cent of the assets managed by the management company or the corresponding Estonian branch;

4) in the case of an insurer providing non-life insurance or reinsurance thereof or an Estonian branch of a foreign company operating as an insurer providing non-life insurance or reinsurance thereof, 0.1 to 0.5 per cent of the gross insurance premiums earned by the insurer or the corresponding Estonian branch. Reinsurance premiums paid to an insurer shall not be included in the total of the insurance premiums if, according to the reinsurance contract, the ceding company is an insurer registered in Estonia;

5) in the case of an insurer providing life insurance or reinsurance thereof or an Estonian branch of a foreign company operating as an insurer providing life insurance or reinsurance thereof, 0.05 to 0.25 per cent of the calculated assets of the insurer or the corresponding Estonian branch.

6) in the case of an insurance broker or an Estonian branch of a foreign company operating as an insurance broker, 1 to 5 per cent of the gross income from the commissions received by the insurance broker or the Estonian branch;

7) in the case of Lloyd's, 0.1 to 0.5 per cent of the gross insurance premiums earned by Lloyd's in Estonia.

(3) For the purposes of this Act, assets are taken to be total assets indicated on the balance sheet as provided by legislation.

(4) For the purposes of this Act, calculated assets are taken to be the total amount of assets and gross insurance premiums.

§ 38. Establishment of rate of share of supervision fee calculated on basis of assets

(1) The rate of the share of the supervision fee calculated on the basis of assets shall be established for a calendar year as a percentage within the limits provided for in subsection 37 (2) of this Act. The rate shall be established by a regulation of the Minister of Finance within ten days after approval of the budget of the Supervisory Authority by the supervisory board.

(2) The rate of the share of the supervision fee calculated on the basis of assets shall be the same for all persons and Estonian branches of foreign companies operating in the same area of activity.

(3) The rate of the share of the supervision fee calculated on the basis of assets shall be applied to calculation of the advance payment and final payment of the supervision fee.

§ 39. Calculation of advance payment of supervision fee on basis of assets and gross insurance premiums

(1) In the case of a credit institution, investment firm or management company, the advance payment of the share of the supervision fee calculated on the basis of assets shall be calculated on the basis of the arithmetic mean of the assets of the person or the corresponding Estonian branch of a foreign company, calculated according to the data on the balance sheet thereof as at 31 December of the preceding year and 31 March and 30 June of the current year.

(2) In the case of an insurer providing life-insurance or reinsurance thereof, the advance payment of the share of the supervision fee calculated on the basis of assets shall be calculated on the basis of the arithmetic mean of the calculated assets of the person or the corresponding Estonian branch of a foreign company, calculated according to the data in the balance sheet and income statement thereof as at 31 December of the preceding year and 31 March and 30 June of the current year.

(3) In the case of Lloyd's, an insurance broker or an insurer providing non-life insurance or reinsurance thereof, the advance payment of the share of the supervision fee calculated on the basis of assets shall be calculated on the basis of twice the amount of the gross insurance premiums earned by the person or the corresponding Estonian branch of a foreign company according to the data presented in the half yearly income statement of the person or branch.

(4) In the event of dissolution, calculation shall be based on the balance sheet prepared upon liquidation.

§ 40. Calculation of final payment of supervision fee on basis of assets and gross insurance premiums

(1) In the case of a credit institution, investment firm or management company, the final payment of the share of the supervision fee calculated on the basis of assets shall be calculated on the basis of the arithmetic mean of the assets of the person or the corresponding Estonian branch of a foreign company, calculated according to the data on the balance sheet thereof as at 31 March, 30 June, 30 September and 31 December of the preceding year.

(2) In the case of an insurer providing life-insurance or reinsurance thereof, the final payment of the share of the supervision fee calculated on the basis of assets shall be calculated on the basis of the arithmetic mean of the calculated assets of the person or the corresponding Estonian branch of a foreign company, calculated according to the data in the balance sheet and income statement thereof as at 31 March, 30 June, 30 September and 31 December of the preceding year.

(3) In the case of Lloyd's, an insurance broker or an insurer providing non-life insurance or reinsurance thereof, the final payment of the share of the supervision fee calculated on the basis of assets shall be calculated on the basis of the gross insurance premiums earned by the person or the corresponding Estonian branch of a foreign company according to the data presented in the previous year's income statement of the person or branch.

(4) If a financing obligation arises during a calendar year, the final payment of the share of the supervision fee calculated on the basis of assets payable for the forthcoming budgetary year shall be calculated on the basis of the assets, calculated assets or gross insurance premiums provided for in subsections (1)–(3) of this section as at 31 December.

(5) In the event of dissolution, calculation shall be based on the balance sheet prepared upon liquidation.

§ 41. Payment of supervision fee

(1) Payment of the supervision fee shall be requested in a corresponding notice sent by the Supervisory Authority.

(2) The supervision fee shall be paid as an advance payment and final payment. The size of the final payment of the supervision fee shall be the final amount of the supervision fee to be paid during a particular budgetary year of the Supervisory Authority (hereinafter budgetary year) for that year.

(3) If an advance payment of the supervision fee exceeds the final payment, the Supervisory Authority shall refund the overpaid amount of the supervision fee by the due date provided for in subsection 42 (2) of this Act.

(4) If an advance payment of the supervision fee is less than the final payment, a final payment in the amount of the difference between the final payment and the

advance payment shall be made by the due date provided for in subsection 42 (2) of this Act.

(5) If a financing obligation arises during the first half of a calendar year, the final payment of the supervision fee shall be made only in the full amount of the capital share. As an exception, an Estonian branch of a foreign company, operating in the area of activity of an investment firm, insurer, insurance broker, credit institution or management company, shall pay the final amount of the supervision fee only in the amount of half the capital share.

(6) If a financing obligation arises during the second half of a calendar year, the final payment of the supervision fee shall be made only in the amount of half the capital share. As an exception, an Estonian branch of a foreign company, operating in the area of activity of an investment firm, insurer, insurance broker, credit institution or management company, shall pay the final amount of the supervision fee only in the amount of one-quarter of the capital share.

(7) The supervision fee shall be paid into the account of the Supervisory Authority in the Bank of Estonia.

§ 42. Term for payment of supervision fee

(1) Any advance payment of the share of the supervision fee calculated on the basis of assets which is payable for a budgetary year shall be made by 31 December of the preceding year.

(2) The final payment of the share of the supervision fee calculated on the basis of assets shall be made by 1 September of the budgetary year.

(3) The capital share of the supervision fee shall be paid in two equal parts by 31 December of the year preceding the budgetary year and by 30 June of the current budgetary year.

(4) If a financing obligation arises during the current year, the capital share of the supervision fee shall be paid within 30 days after the obligation has arisen.

§ 43. Consequences of failure to pay supervision fee

(1) If a person fails to pay the supervision fee to the Supervisory Authority by the due date provided for in § 42 of this Act or fails to pay the fee in full, the Supervisory Authority shall send a claim for enforcement to the relevant agency, body or person. Enforcement proceedings with regard to such decision shall be commenced immediately after service of the enforcement document on the person who failed to pay the supervision fee in part or in full.

(2) Enforcement proceedings commenced on the basis of subsection (1) of this section may be suspended, enforcement may be extended or postponed and the method of and procedure for the enforcement may be amended only on the basis of a court judgment which has entered into force or a petition of the claimant.

§ 44. Budgetary year of Supervisory Authority
The budgetary year of the Supervisory Authority begins on 1 January and ends on 31 December.

§ 45. Supplementary budget of Supervisory Authority
(1) A supplementary budget shall be drawn up if the budgetary funds are not sufficient to cover the extraordinary expenses incurred by the Supervisory Authority during a budgetary year.

(2) A draft supplementary budget shall be drawn up by the management board who shall submit the draft to the supervisory board for approval.

Chapter 5

Co-operation

§ 46. Co-operation with international organizations
The Supervisory Authority shall participate in and co-operate with international organizations within the limits of its competence.

§ 47. Co-operation with foreign financial supervision authorities
(1) The Supervisory Authority shall co-operate with foreign financial supervision authorities and other competent foreign bodies or persons.

(2) The Supervisory Authority has the right to send confidential information necessary for the performance of its functions to the subjects of co-operation specified in subsection (1) of this section and to obtain such information therefrom and exchange such information therewith. Information sent, received or exchanged in this manner is deemed to be confidential.

(3) The Supervisory Authority has the right to communicate confidential information to a foreign financial supervision authority or other competent foreign body or person only if the receiver of the confidential information is obliged to maintain the confidentiality of the information received and the information is used only for the purposes of financial supervision. The Supervisory Authority may use information received on the basis of subsection (2) of this section only for the purposes of financial supervision.

(4) Information received as a result of the co-operation specified in subsection (1) of this section may be disclosed in the cases provided for in clauses 54 (4) 1)–6) of this Act if a corresponding agreement has been entered into with the foreign financial supervision authority or other competent foreign authority or person.

§ 48. Provision of information

(1) The Supervisory Authority has the right to obtain information necessary for the performance of its functions from the Bank of Estonia, the Ministry of Finance and other state agencies.

(2) The Supervisory Authority is required to provide the Bank of Estonia and the Ministry of Finance with information necessary for the performance of their functions.

§ 49. Co-operation of Supervisory Authority with Bank of Estonia, Ministry of Finance and other state agencies in field of legislative drafting

(1) The Supervisory Authority shall submit a report on the effects and application of legislation relating to the financial sector and financial supervision to the Government of the Republic and the Bank of Estonia by 1 October each year.

(2) The Supervisory Authority has the right to submit proposals to the Bank of Estonia, the Ministry of Finance and other state agencies concerning the drafting, amendment and repeal of legislation.

(3) If a legal act to be drafted or amended by the Bank of Estonia, the Ministry of Finance or any other state agency regulates the activities of a subject of financial supervision or the Supervisory Authority or has any other impact on the attainment of the objectives of financial supervision, the draft act shall be co-ordinated with the Supervisory Authority.

§ 50. Co-operation agreements

(1) The Supervisory Authority may enter into a bilateral or multilateral agreement for co-operation with the Bank of Estonia, the Ministry of Finance or any other state agency if such co-operation is necessary to promote attainment of the objectives of financial supervision.

(2) The Supervisory Authority, the Ministry of Finance and the Bank of Estonia shall, on the basis of a written agreement, co-operate in the collection and analysis of reporting, the drafting of legislation and the exchange of information in the case of events which have a substantial impact on the situation in the financial sector.

Chapter 6

Reporting and Disclosure of Activities

§ 51. Annual report

(1) The annual report of the Supervisory Authority consists of the management report, the statement of revenue and expenditure, and the auditor's report.

(2) The supervisory board shall approve the annual report of the Supervisory Authority within three months as of the end of the budgetary year.

(3) The statement of revenue and expenditure of the Supervisory Authority shall be audited by an auditor of the Bank of Estonia.

(4) The annual report of the Supervisory Authority approved by the supervisory board shall be submitted to the Riigikogu[2] together with the annual report of the Bank of Estonia. The Riigikogu shall hear the report of the chairman of the management board concerning the annual report of the Supervisory Authority pursuant to the procedure prescribed by the Riigikogu Rules of Procedure Act (RT I 1994, 90, 1517; 2001, 1, 1).

§ 52. Yearbook of Supervisory Authority

(1) Every year, the Supervisory Authority shall publish a yearbook of the Supervisory Authority.

(2) The yearbook of the Supervisory Authority shall contain the annual report of the Supervisory Authority approved by the supervisory board, a list of the advisory guidelines issued by the Supervisory Authority and the relevant explanations, and a summary report of the activities of the subjects of financial supervision during the previous calendar year.

§ 53. Disclosure of activities of Supervisory Authority

(1) The Supervisory Authority shall publish the resolutions of the supervisory board on its web site. Resolutions containing information specified in clauses 7 (2) 7) or 8) or subsection 54 (2) of this Act, with the exception of information concerning circumstances relating to the termination of the contract of service of the chairman of the management board, are not public information.

(2) Resolutions of the management board are not public information and they shall be disclosed only in the cases and pursuant to the procedure provided in the Acts specified in § 2 of this Act.

(3) The advisory guidelines issued by the Supervisory Authority on the basis of § 57 of this Act shall be published on its web site.

(4) The Supervisory Authority shall publish the lists provided for in the Acts specified in subsection 2 (1) of this Act and other information subject to disclosure on its web site.

§ 54. Confidentiality of information received during supervision

(1) Proceedings conducted by the Supervisory Authority for the conduct of financial supervision shall not be public.

(2) Information obtained in the course of financial supervision from the subjects of financial supervision or other persons or agencies, including data, documents and other information, certificates, reports and precepts prepared in the course of

---

2 Riigikogu = the parliament of Estonia

financial supervision, and other documents and any type of data media containing information on the results of financial supervision shall be confidential.

(3) Information is not confidential if it has been published pursuant to the procedure prescribed in the Acts specified in subsection 2 (1) of this Act or legislation established on the basis thereof or if the information disclosed does not enable data concerning specific persons to be ascertained.

(4) Confidential information specified in subsection (2) of this section and documents containing information on the results of financial supervision may be disclosed to:

1) courts and investigative bodies in connection with acts detected during financial supervision or the acts of a subject of financial supervision or the head or an employee thereof if such acts contain elements of a criminal offence;

2) administrative courts in matters relating to the conduct of financial supervision;

3) employees of the Bank of Estonia and public servants of the Ministry of Finance if this is necessary for the performance of their duties, on the condition that they are required to maintain professional secrets pursuant to law;

4) a court, liquidator of a subject of financial supervision, interim trustee or trustee in bankruptcy in the liquidation or bankruptcy proceedings of a subject of financial supervision, and to a moratorium administrator of a credit institution or special regime trustee of an insurance company to the extent necessary for the performance of their duties;

5) the Deposit Guarantee Fund to the extent necessary for the performance of its functions;

6) the auditor of a subject of financial supervision to the extent necessary for the activities of the auditor;

7) a foreign financial supervision authority in the case specified in § 47 of this Act.

Chapter 7

Legal Acts and Liability

§ 55. Resolutions and precepts of management board

(1) The management board shall adopt resolutions and issue precepts on the bases and pursuant to the procedure provided for in this Act and the Acts specified in § 2 of this Act.

(2) An appeal may be filed with an administrative court against a resolution or precept of the management board or a financial supervision operation on the bases and pursuant to the procedure prescribed by law.

§ 56. Precepts of chairman of management board

The chairman of the management board shall issue directives to regulate matters relating to the internal organization of the activities and the management of the Supervisory Authority.

§ 57. Guidelines of Supervisory Authority

(1) The Supervisory Authority has the right to issue advisory guidelines to explain legislation regulating the activities of the financial sector and to provide guidance to subjects of financial supervision.

(2) The Supervisory Authority has the right to involve experts and representatives of the subjects of financial supervision in the drafting of advisory guidelines.

(3) The advisory guidelines of the Supervisory Authority shall be approved by a resolution of the management board and the guidelines shall be disclosed as provided for in subsection 53 (3) of this Act.

§ 58. Liability of Supervisory Authority

(1) The liability of the Supervisory Authority for rights violated or damage caused in the conduct of financial supervision, and the bases of and procedure for the restoration of violated rights and the payment of compensation for damage caused shall be provided by law.

(2) The Supervisory Authority shall be liable for damage not related to the conduct of financial supervision pursuant to the provisions of private law and within the limits of the funds prescribed in its budget. If the funds prescribed in the budget of the Supervisory Authority are not sufficient, the damage shall be compensated for by the Bank of Estonia.

Chapter 8

Implementing Provisions

§ 59. Commencement of activities of Supervisory Authority

The Supervisory Authority shall commence activities on 1 January 2002.

§ 60. Appointment of members of supervisory board and management board

(1) The Government of the Republic and the Board of the Bank of Estonia shall appoint the members of the supervisory board within one month after the entry into force of this Act.

(2) The Minister of Finance shall call the first meeting of the supervisory board within twenty days after all members of the supervisory board have been appointed.

(3) The agenda of the first meeting of the supervisory board shall include at least the election of the chairman of the management board from among the persons specified in subsection 61 (1) of this Act.

(4) The supervisory board shall appoint the members of the management board pursuant to the procedure provided by this Act not later than by 30 June 2002.

§ 61. Commencement of activities of Supervisory Authority

(1) The Director General of the Securities Inspectorate, the Director General of the Insurance Supervisory Authority and the Head of the Banking Supervision of the Bank of Estonia, or the persons performing their duties, shall perform the duties of a member of the management board provided by this Act if, by 10 June 2001, they have granted corresponding written consent to the person or body who appointed them. If one of the aforementioned persons refuses to consent, he or she shall be released from service on the basis of § 116 of the Public Service Act (RT I 1995, 16, 228; 1999, 7, 112; 10, 155; 16, 271 and 276; 2000, 25, 144 and 145; 28, 167; 102, 672; 2001, 7, 17 and 18; 17, 78; 42, 233) or the employment contract with him or her shall be terminated on the basis of clause 86 3) of the Republic of Estonia Employment Contracts Act.

(2) The term of the authority of the persons specified in subsection (1) of this section commences on the day following the date of the first meeting of the supervisory board and ends upon commencement of the term of the authority of the members of the management board pursuant to the procedure provided for in subsection 21 (3) of this Act.

(3) Until the term of the authority of the members of the management board provided for in subsection 60 (4) of this Act commences, the management board shall consist of three members.

(4) The management board consisting of the persons specified in subsection (1) of this section (hereinafter the management board) has a quorum if all members of the management board are present. A resolution of the management board is adopted if at least two members of the management board vote in favor.

(5) The management board shall, pursuant to the procedure established by the supervisory board, report to the supervisory board on the implementation of the action plan for commencement of the activities of the Supervisory Authority.

§ 62. Continuation or termination of service or employment relationships

(1) Officials of the Securities Inspectorate and the Insurance Supervisory Authority and employees of the Banking Supervision of the Bank of Estonia who meet the requirements for employees provided by this Act and who submit a corresponding application to the management board by 1 November 2001 shall be employed by the Supervisory Authority as of 1 January 2002. In such case, the

service relationship of an official of the Securities Inspectorate or the Insurance Supervisory Authority shall be deemed to terminate as of 31 December 2001 on the basis of § 114 of the Public Service Act.

(2) Officials of the Securities Inspectorate and the Insurance Supervisory Authority and employees of the Banking Supervision of the Bank of Estonia who do not meet the requirements for employees provided by this Act or who do not submit the application specified in subsection (1) of this section shall be released from service on the basis of § 116 of the Public Service Act or the employment contracts with such persons shall be terminated on the basis of clause 86 3) of the Republic of Estonia Employment Contracts Act.

(3) The length of service of a person at the Financial Supervisory Authority shall be calculated as of the commencement of his or her employment or service at the Bank of Estonia, the Insurance Supervisory Authority or the Securities Inspectorate.

§ 63. Transfer of assets and performance of proprietary obligations
(1) State assets in the possession and at the disposal of the Securities Inspectorate or the Insurance Supervisory Authority which are necessary for the activities of the Supervisory Authority shall be transferred by the administrator of state assets to the Supervisory Authority free of charge not later than by 1 January 2002.

(2) The state shall be liable with the budgetary funds thereof for proprietary obligations which arise out of the activities of the Securities Inspectorate or the Insurance Supervisory Authority before 1 January 2002, and the Bank of Estonia shall be liable with the budgetary funds thereof for proprietary obligations which arise out of the activities of the Banking Supervision of the Bank of Estonia before 1 January 2002.

§ 64. Application of Act
(1) Administrative matters and administrative offence matters which are subject to proceeding by the Securities Inspectorate, the Insurance Supervisory Authority or the Banking Supervision of the Bank of Estonia on 1 January 2002 and petitions which have been submitted but not accepted by that date shall be transferred to the Supervisory Authority who shall conclude the proceedings pursuant to this Act and the Acts specified in subsection 2 (1) of this Act.

(2) In matters arising from the conduct of supervision over securities markets or insurance activities, which are subject to court proceeding as at 1 January 2002 and in which the state is represented by the Securities Inspectorate or the Insurance Supervisory Authority on the basis of law or general or special authorization or in which one of the participants in the proceedings is the Bank of Estonia in a dispute concerning the exercise of banking supervision, the state shall be

thereafter represented by the Supervisory Authority or the Supervisory Authority shall substitute for the Bank of Estonia as a participant in the proceedings.

(3) Activity licenses and authorisations, other permits and administrative legislation of specific application issued by competent bodies on the basis of an Act specified in § 2 of this Act before the commencement of the activities of the Supervisory Authority shall be valid until the expiry thereof or until their revocation.

(4) In 2002 and 2003, the expenses of the Supervisory Authority may be partially covered from the funds prescribed in the budget of the Bank of Estonia or from the appropriations prescribed in the state budget.

(5) If the expenses of the Supervisory Authority are partially covered on the basis of subsection (4) of this section, rates of the supervision fee lower than the rates provided for in § 37 of this Act may be applied.

§ 65. Information relating to supervision activities
(1) Information relating to the supervision activities of the Securities Inspectorate, the Insurance Supervisory Authority or the Banking Supervision of the Bank of Estonia which is recorded or documented in any manner on any data media shall be transferred to the Supervisory Authority.

(2) A member of the management board or an employee of the Supervisory Authority may disclose confidential information obtained in the course of the supervision activities of the Securities Inspectorate, the Insurance Supervisory Authority or the Banking Supervision to other members of the management board or employees of the Supervisory Authority if this is necessary for the performance of their duties.

§ 66. Entry into force of Act
(1) This Act enters into force on 1 June 2001.

(2) Clauses 7 (2) 4)–7), subsection 14 (5), subsection 18 (2), clauses 18 (3) 3), 4), 8), 10) and 13)–15), §§ 20–22, 29, 51 and 52, subsection 53 (3) and §§ 54, 55, 57 and 58 of this Act enter into force on 1 January 2002.

(3) Subsection 53 (4) of this Act enters into force on 1 July 2002.

The Hungarian Financial Supervisory
Authority Act, 1999[*]

Chapter I

The Legal Status, Powers and Tasks of the Hungarian Financial Supervisory Authority

Article 1

(1) The Hungarian Financial Supervisory Authority (hereinafter: Supervision) is a national public administration organisation, operating under direction by the Government, supervised by the Minister of Finance.

(2) The Supervision is a budget agency endowed with budget chapter management powers, the budget of which is separated within the chapter of the Ministry of Finance.

(3) The Supervision shall be headquartered in Budapest.

(4) Tasks for the Supervision may be assigned only by law or by legislation drafted on the basis of authorisation granted in a law. The Supervision may not be instructed in terms of its tasks specified in laws.

Article 2

(1) The aim of the Supervision's activities shall be to promote and monitor the undisturbed and effective operation of the money and capital market, the protection of the interests of financial organisations' clients, the transparency of market conditions, the strengthening of confidence in financial markets, and in order to maintain fair market competition, to promote and monitor the prudent and efficient operation of organisations or persons pursuing financial service, auxiliary financial service, clearing house, investment management, commodity exchange service, insurance, insurance brokerage, insurance consulting activities, voluntary mutual insurance funds, private pension funds, public warehouses, venture capital companies, venture capital funds, venture capital fund managers as well as exchanges and their members (hereinafter collectively: financial organisations) and the careful exercising of rights by the owners of the above.

---

[*] Unofficial translation, available at, <http://www.pszaf.hu/english/intro/laws.htm>.

(2) The Supervision will continuously monitor compliance with the legislation and Supervision regulations applicable to the operation of financial organisations, and shall have the power to take measures specified in separate law and will propose proceedings to other organisations having the relevant powers in case such regulations—particularly the requirements concerning money laundering, insider trading, unfair price manipulation—are violated.

Article 3
The scope of the power of the Supervision shall extend to the supervision of organisations, persons and activities covered by:

a) Act No. CXII of 1996 on credit institutions and financial enterprises (hereinafter: Hpt);

b) Act CXX of 2001 on capital markets (hereinafter: Tpt.)

c)

d)

e) Act XCVI of 1995 on insurance companies and insurance activities (hereinafter: Bit);

f) Act XCVI of 1993 on Mutual Voluntary Insurance Funds;

g) Act LXXXII of 1997 on private pension and private pension funds;

h) Act XLVIII of 1996 on public warehousing;

i) the various acts on certain specialised credit institutions;

j) Act XXXIV of 1998 on venture capital investments and venture capital funds.

Article 4
(1) The Supervision shall perform all of the responsibilities assigned to it by the law or by any statute issued under authorisation by the law.

(2) The provisions of Act No. IV of 1957 on the general rules of public administration proceedings shall be applied to the procedures of the Supervision with the differences laid out herein and in the acts listed in art 3.

(3) Resolutions made by the Supervision may not be altered, modified or annulled within supervisory powers and there is no appeal against them through public administration procedures.

(4) The Supervision shall have the right to comment in the course of preparing legislation involving the finance system and the institutions and persons supervised, and will make proposals on the drafting of legislation. The Supervision's comments shall be sought in respect of drafts of decisions and legislation involving the finance system and the supervised institutions.

(5)

(6) Claim for damages may be enforced against the Supervision—on account of its resolutions made by the Supervision as an authority—only if the resolution or failure of action on the part of the Supervision has violated the law and the damage suffered by such claimant has been directly caused by the resolution or failure of the Supervision.

(7) The President of the Supervision may issue guidelines covering the basic principles of legal enforcement applied by the Supervision. The guidelines have no legally binding obligation in regard of organizations, persons subjected to Acts listed under Article 3, its purpose is to enhance the predictability of legal enforcement.

International co-operation

Article 5

(1) The Supervision may perform co-operation agreements and may exchange information with foreign financial supervision agencies in order to perform its tasks and to promote the implementation of consolidated supervision as well as integration processes.

(2) The Supervision may join international organisations promoting the international co-operation between financial supervision agencies as a member.

(3) The Supervision may use individual data and information received from foreign financial supervision agencies in the course of international co-operation only for the following purposes and may release data to foreign financial supervision agencies only for the following purposes:

a) for evaluating applications for the licencing of establishment or operation of financial organisations and for verifying the contents of licences, for evaluating the prudent operation of organisations,

b) for use as grounds for the Supervision's resolutions, particularly actions or sanctions.

(4) Individual data and information provided or obtained in the framework of co-operation between supervision agencies may be disclosed to third parties only with the prior written consent of the supervision that provided the data.

(5) Supervision information and data may be released to foreign supervision agencies only if the foreign partner is able to guarantee appropriate legal protection that is at least equivalent to Hungarian regulations for handling the information provided to it.

Disclosure of resolutions

Article 6

(1) While observing bank and securities secrecy, fund secrecy, insurance secrecy and business secret the Supervision shall be entitled to disclose parts or the whole

of its resolutions in the Financial Gazette (Pénzügyi Közlöny) and in other modes considered by the Supervision as expedient, in order to ensure the protection of the participants of the money and capital market, investors, deposit holders, insureds or members of funds.

(2) In the Financial Gazette the Supervision shall regularly disclose

a) the list of entities holding operating licences issued by the Supervision;

b) the list of foreign supervisory authorities with which the Supervision has concluded co-operation agreements based on mutual recognition.

Chapter II

The Supervision's Relationships with Other Organizations

Relationship with the Parliament

Article 6/A
The President of the Supervision shall inform the competent committee of the Parliament—following the report provided to the Government—each year about the Supervision's activities.

Relationship with the Government and Ministries

Article 6/B
(1) The President of the Supervision shall report to the Government about the Supervision's authorities by the 30 September of each year, and will publish information on the Supervision's operation at the same time.

(2) The President of the Supervision shall be invited to attend the Government's sessions in respect of agenda items concerning the Supervision's tasks.

Relationship with the National Bank of Hungary

Article 6/C
(1) In the course of performing its tasks the Supervision shall co-operate with the National Bank of Hungary (hereinafter: NBH).

(2) In the cases specified by law the Supervision shall issue or withdraw licences after requesting preliminary opinion or agreement from NBH.

Chapter III

Executives and Employees of the Supervision

Article 7
(1) The Supervision is headed by the President who has two Deputy Presidents.

(2) The President of the Supervision will be elected for a period of six years or recalled by the Parliament on the Prime Minister's proposal. The competent committee of the Parliament will hear the person proposed. The two Deputy Presidents of the Supervision will be appointed for a period of six years or released from office by the Prime Minister. The proposal concerning appointment or releasing from office will be made by the President of the Supervision, and submitted to the Prime Minister by the Minister of Finance (if he agrees to the proposal).

(3) In respect of the President and Deputy President of the Supervision the rights of the employer shall be exercised by the Minister of Finance on behalf of the Government, with the exception as per paragraph (2).

(4) The appointment of the Supervision's President will be terminated:

    a) when the term of appointment expires

    b) with resignation

    c) with recalling from office

    d) when a conflict of interest is established

    e) by death.

(5) Resignation shall be communicated in writing to the President of the Parliament and to the Prime Minister.

(6) The appointment

    a) may be terminated by recalling if the President of the Supervision is not able to perform his tasks arising out of his appointment for a reason that may not be attributed to him

    b) shall be terminated by recalling if the President of the Supervision fails to perform his tasks arising out of his appointment for a reason that is attributable to him or a final and enforceable court verdict finds that he has committed an act of crime.

(7) If the appointment of the Supervision's President is terminated by recalling, the reasons for recalling shall be communicated to the public.

(8) If the reason for conflict of interest set out in Article 10 exists in connection with the Supervision's President he shall terminate it within 10 days of his appointment. He may not exercise his powers arising out of his position until this takes place.

(9) If the Supervision's President fails to perform the obligation set out in section (8) by the deadline specified above the Parliament will establish that there is a conflict of interest in a resolution.

(10) Section (4) of this Article—except for sub-section d) of that section—and sections (6) and (7) shall apply also in respect of the Supervision's

Deputy Presidents with the difference that recalling shall read as releasing from office and the resignation shall be communicated in writing to the Prime Minister.

(11) With the exceptions stipulated in this Act, the provisions set forth in the frequently amended Act XXIII of 1992 on the Legal Status of Civil Servants (hereinafter by the Hungarian abbreviation: Ktv.) shall be observed with regard to the President, the Deputy Presidents and the Supervision's staff, whereby

a) for the purposes of sub-section b) of Section (1) of Article 8 and Section (2) of Article 30/A of Ktv., employment with a financial organization supervised by the Supervision shall be recognized as administrative experience;

b) the percentage specified in Section (1) of Article 30/A of Ktv. shall be thirty-five percent;

(12) The Supervision may appoint managing directors as well, providing that a managing director shall be a person in a position ranking as head of department, carrying out the tasks of the management of several departments.

Article 8

The President of the Supervision shall

a) direct the working organisation of the Supervision;

b) exercise the rights of the employer in respect of the employees of the Supervision;

c) direct the financial management of the Supervision;

d) represent the Supervision;

e) perform the tasks assigned to his scope of competency by law or by the organisation and operation rules of the Supervision.

f) participates—with the right of consulting—at the meetings of Government discussing issues relating to the responsibilities of the Supervision.

Article 9

(1) The requirements to be met by the person to be elected/appointed President or Deputy President of the Supervision include higher academic qualification in relevant fields and at least five years of managerial (executive) working experience acquired in a financial organisation or in public administration in the regulation or controlling of financial organisations, or equivalent working experience acquired abroad.

(2) Higher academic qualifications in relevant fields include degree obtained at the university of political sciences and law, university of economics, college of state administration or college of finance and accounting.

Revenue of the President and Deputy Presidents of the Supervision
Article 9/A

(1) The total annual revenue of the Supervision's President shall correspond to the total revenue of NBH's President received from NBH.

(2) The total annual revenue for Deputy Presidents shall correspond to eighty per cent of the total revenue of NBH's President received from NBH.

Supervision Council

Article 9/B

(1) The Supervision Council is an advisory body for the President having fifteen members. Sessions of the Council will be chaired by the Supervision's President.

(2) The Supervision's President will appoint council members based on consultations with the Minister of Finance in respect of one-third of members and with the professional associations representing the sector supervised in respect of two-thirds of members, out of persons having outstanding theoretical and practical professional knowledge of the issues related to the activities of financial organisations.

(3) The Supervision Council will express its positions on the issues of principle relevant for the strategic further development and the Supervision as well as of the regulation and its application and further development.

(4) The members shall be appointed for 3 years.

Conflict of interest

Article 10

(1) No legal relationship of civil service may be established at the Supervision if the civil servant concerned would thereby establish a relationship of governance (supervision) controlling or settlement with a close relative of such civil servant in a public service relationship with the Supervision.

(2) Civil servants of the Supervision may not enter membership, employment or other legal relationship that entails working, executive employment or supervisory board membership—except for Article 110 section (2) sub-section c) of the Hpt.—with the National Deposit Insurance Fund and the Investor Protection Fund. This prohibition shall not be infringed if the civil servant is a member of a voluntary mutual insurance fund and private pension fund or insurance society. The civil servant of the Supervision may be assigned as a member of the supervisory board of non-profit companies specified in Hpt.

(3) A civil servant of the Supervision shall not acquire the following (with the exception of inheritance)

a) ownership in a financial organisation;

b) securities except for domestic and foreign government securities, deposit bonds, investment units, mortgage bonds and securities issued in restricted offering,

c) other investment instruments not listed in sub-section (b) (Article 82 of the Tpt.)

(4) A civil servant of the Supervision shall not hold a share of ownership in a financial organisation, upon his or her appointment he or she shall make a statement to the person exercising the right of employer concerning his or her share of ownership in a financial organisation and on any other investment asset he or she holds which must not be acquired following his or her appointment.

(5) A civil servant of the Supervision shall be obliged to alienate within 3 months of his or her appointment or acquisition all of his or her shares of ownership, securities and any other investment asset, acquired before his or her appointment or acquired through inheritance, as defined in paragraph (3).

(6) A civil servant of the Supervision shall report to the person exercising the right of the employer immediately the acquisition by his or her close relation living in the same household with such civil servant, of any share of ownership, securities or other investment assets as defined in paragraph (3).

(7) Until the performance of his or her obligation as per paragraph (5) and in the case specified in paragraph (6) a civil servant of the Supervision shall not participate in the preparation and making of a decision pertaining to the organisation concerned.

(8) Upon his or her appointment a civil servant of the Supervision shall make a statement on his or her membership in a co-operative credit institution. A civil servant of the Supervision shall not need to terminate his or her membership existing at the time of his or her employment until he or she owes a debt to the credit institution concerned. During this period, however he or she shall not participate in the preparation and making of a decision pertaining to the organisation of which he or she is a member.

(9) Upon his or her appointment a civil servant of the Supervision shall make a written statement on his or her membership in an insurance association or private pension fund. A civil servant of the Supervision shall not participate in the preparation and making of a decision pertaining to the organisation of which he or she is a member.

(10) Upon his or her appointment a civil servant of the Supervision shall make a written statement on his or her close relation living in the same household with him or her having a legal relationship with a financial organisation as a senior executive or employment, or other legal relationship relating to the performance

of work, and any such legal relationship that is established after the appointment of the given civil servant shall be promptly reported to the person exercising the rights of the employer. A civil servant of the Supervision shall not participate in the preparation and making of a decision pertaining to an organisation in which his or her close relation living in the same household with him or her has a legal relationship as listed above.

(11) The civil servant of the Supervision may acquire investment units, securities issued in restricted offering and mortgage bonds in a manner regulated by the person who exercises employer's rights over him.

(12) In respect of the application of this Article close relations shall be the persons defined as such in Article 685 b) of the Civil Code along with the life companion of a civil servant of the Supervision.

(13) Other rules on conflict of interest may be introduced by separate statutes of law.

(14) The President and Deputy Presidents of the Supervision may not fill office in political parties, may not conduct activities that entail playing a public role on behalf or in the interest of a party, and may not be members of Parliament or municipality assemblies, municipality or government executives.

(15) The persons mentioned in section (14) may not be executives of or members of the supervisory board of business companies.

Article 10/A

(1) The Supervision operates a public information system in order to make the information to be supplied by the organisations and persons specified in Article 3 of this Act to the public and the Supervision accessible for the public.

(2) The public information system shall be an electronic system and a daily newspaper published in printed form.

Obligation of secrecy

Article 11

(1) Persons employed or having other legal relationship entailing work or having an assignment from the Supervision shall preserve banking secrets, securities secrets, cashier secrets, insurance secrets and business secrets obtained in the course of performing their tasks as secrets. This obligation shall survive also after the termination of employment or assignment.

(2) Persons listed in section (1) shall treat as professional secrets all data, facts or circumstances obtained in connection with performing supervisory activities that the Supervision is not obliged to make accessible for other authorities or the public, may not disclose without authorisation and may not use in accordance with legal requirements.

Chapter IV

Business Management of the Supervision

Article 11/A

(1) The following items, specified in separate laws, shall constitute the Supervision's revenues:

    a) fee for administrative services

    b) supervision fee

    c) supervisory fine

    d) other revenue.

(2) The organisations and persons which/who are subject to the scope of the laws specified in Article 3 section (1) shall pay fees for administrative services and supervision fees at a specified rate as well as fines in cases defined by law. Based on authorisations granted in separate laws the Minister of Finance will determine the rates of fees for administrative services in a decree. The Minister of Finance shall take into account the opinion of the Supervision's President concerning the issue of increasing or decreasing fees. The fees shall ensure that the Supervision's operation is continuous and undisturbed."e;

Article 11/B

(1) The Supervision will manage its revenue from fees on its own, and the proportion of fines that may be used up will be governed by the provisions of separate laws.

(2) The Supervision will use its revenue—except for revenue out of fines—to cover its operation and such revenue may not be removed for other purposes.

(3) Regarding the budget of the Supervision the President of the Supervision has the powers as the Head of the organization for this Chapter of State Budget under Article 49 of the Act No. XXXVIII of 1992 on State Budget.

Interim and closing provisions

Article 12

(1) This Act shall enter into force on 1 April 2000.

(2) The Hungarian Banking and Capital Markets Supervision, the State Insurance Supervision and the State Supervision of Private Pension Funds shall be dissolved as of 1 April—from that day the Hungarian Financial Supervisory Authority shall be the legal successor of those organisations.

(3) Where the law mentions the Hungarian Banking and Capital Markets Supervision, the State Insurance Supervision and the State Supervision of Funds or

Supervision of Funds they shall be construed as the Hungarian Financial Supervisory Authority as defined herein.

(4) Issues in progress at the time of the entry into force hereof at the Hungarian Banking and Capital Markets Supervision, the State Insurance Supervision and the State Supervision of Funds shall be continued by the Supervision. In the course of such proceedings the procedural rules pertaining to the supervisory authority with competency at the time of the launching of such issues, shall apply.

(5) It shall not constitute breach of the obligation of keeping business secrecy if the State Insurance Supervision, the State Supervision of Funds or the Hungarian Banking and Capital Markets Supervision provide business secrets to one another in the period of the preparation of the establishment of the Hungarian Financial Supervisory Authority.

(6) A civil servant of the Supervision who was in a civil servant legal relation with the State Insurance Supervision or the State Supervision of Funds shall be obliged to promptly report on his or her share of ownership, securities or other investments as per Article 10 (3) to the person exercising the right of the employer and shall be obliged to alienate such within 6 months of the entry into force hereof. Until the alienation of any share of ownership or investment contrary to Article 10 (3) such civil servant shall not participate in the preparation or making of a decision that pertains to an institution in which such share of ownership or investment exists.

Statutes of law amended

Article 13

(1) In Article 8 of Act No. XCVI of 1993 on voluntary mutual insurance funds, the text 'the Minister of Finance by way of the Supervision of Funds' shall be replaced by the text 'Hungarian Financial Supervisory Authority'.

(2) In Article 101 of Act No. LXXXII of 1997 on private pension and private pension funds, the text '... supervision shall be performed by the Minister of Finance—through the Supervision of Funds -' shall be replaced by the text '... supervision shall be performed by the Hungarian Financial Supervisory Authority'.

(3) Article 103 of the Bit shall be replaced by the following provision:

'Article 103 The scope of competency and legal status of the Supervision shall be specified by a separate act.'

(4) Article 102 of Act No. LXXII of 1997 on voluntary mutual insurance funds shall be replaced with the following provision:

'Article 103 The scope of competency and legal status of the Supervision shall be specified by a separate act.'

(5) Article 121 (1) a) of the Bit shall be replaced with the following provision:

[(1) The obligation of secrecy as per Article 120 shall not extend to the following]

'a) data provision to the National Bank of Hungary on its written request'.

(6) The list in Article 44 (2) of Act XXIII of 1992 on the legal status of civil servants shall be supplemented with the Hungarian Financial Supervisory Authority.

Statutes of law abrogated

Article 14

Upon the entry into fore hereof the following shall be abrogated:

a) Act No. CXIV of 1996 on the State Banking and Capital Markets Supervision;

b) Article 41 of Act No. XXXIX of 1998 on venture capital investments, venture capital companies and venture capital funds;

c) Article 104, Article 105 (1)-(2), Article 119, Article 122 (1) and (3) of the Bit;

d) In Article 104(1)-(3) and (5)-(7), Article 195, Article 121(2)d) of Act No. LXXXII of 1997 on private pension and private pension funds the text 'State Banking and Capital Markets Supervision';

e) the second and third sentences of Article 3(5) and Article 196 of the Hpt;

f) Article 66 of Act LXVIII of 1997 on the amendment of the Hpt.

The Latvian Law on the Financial and Capital Market Commission 2001*

Passed on June 1, 2000

In effect as of July 1, 2001
Note.

This Law will be effective as of July 1, 2001, except for Article 13, on the appointment of Chairperson and his/her Deputy, and Items 1, 2, and 4 of the Transitional Provisions that are effective as of the day following its promulgation.

With amendments passed by the Saeima (Parliament) on 8 November 2001, which took effect on 1 January 2002 (*).

Section I

General Provisions

Article 1
This Law shall specify the provisions for the establishment and operation of the Financial and Capital Market Commission (hereinafter, the Commission).

Article 2
(1) The Commission shall enjoy full rights of an independent/autonomous public institution and, in compliance with its goals and objectives, shall regulate and monitor the functioning of the financial and capital market and its participants.

(2) The Commission shall make independent decisions within the limits of its authority, execute functions assigned to it by law, and be responsible for their execution. No one shall be entitled to interfere with the activities of the Commission, except institutions and officials authorised by law.

Article 3
(1) The Commission's legal ability and capacity shall comply with the objectives set forth in this and other laws. The Commission shall be assigned property owned by the state and have an independent balance sheet.

---

* Unofficial translation, available at <http://www.fktk.lv/law/general/laws/article.php?id=20892>.

(2) The Commission shall have a seal bearing its full name, other corporate requisites and an account with the Bank of Latvia.

Article 4

Participants in the financial and capital market shall be issuers, investors, credit institutions, insurers, private pension funds, insurance brokers, stock exchanges, depositories, broker companies, brokers, investment companies, credit unions and investment consultants (*).

Section II

Commission's Goals, Functions, Authorities and Responsibilities

Article 5

The goal of the Commission's activities shall be to protect the interests of investors, depositors and the insured, and to promote the development and stability of the financial and capital market.

Article 6

The Commission shall have the following functions:

1) to issue binding rules and regulations and directives setting out requirements for the functioning of financial and capital market participants and calculation and reporting of their performance indicators;

2) by controlling compliance with regulatory requirements and directives issued by the Commission, to regulate activities of financial and capital market participants;

3) to specify the qualification and conformity requirement for financial and capital market participants and their officials;

4) to establish the procedure for licensing and registration of financial and capital market participants;

5) to collect and analyse information (data) relating to the financial and capital market and to publish it;

6) to ensure accumulation of funds with the Deposit Guarantee Fund, and Protection Fund for the Insured, their management and payment of compensation from these funds in accordance with the Laws on Deposits of Individuals and the Insurance Companies and their Supervision;

7) (*) to ensure payment of compensations to investors in accordance with the Investor Protection Law;

8) to analyse regulatory requirements pertaining to financial and capital market and draft proposals for their improvement and harmonisation with the regulatory requirements Community;

9) to engage in systemic studies, analysis and forecasting of the financial and capital market development;

10) to cooperate with foreign financial and capital market supervision authorities and participate in international organizations of the financial and capital market supervision institutions.

Article 7

(1) Executing the functions specified under Article 6 hereof, the Commission shall have authority:

1) to issue regulations and directives, governing activities of financial and capital market participants;

2) to request and receive information necessary for the execution of its functions from financial and capital market participants;

3) to, in cases stipulated under the regulations, set forth restrictions on the activities of financial and capital market participants;

4) to examine compliance of the activities of financial and capital market participants with the legislation, and regulations and directives of the Commission;

5) to apply sanctions set forth by the regulatory requirement to financial and capital market participants and their officials in case said requirements are violated;

6) to participate in the general meeting of financial and capital market participants to initiate convening of meetings of financial and capital market participants' management bodies, specify items for their agenda, and participate therein;

7) to request and receive, from the Commercial Register and other public institutions, any information required for execution of its functions free of charge;

8) to cooperate with foreign financial and capital market supervision authorities and, upon mutual consent, exchange information necessary to execute its functions set forth by law;

(2) In order to execute its functions specified by law, the Commission is entitled to carry out other activities permitted under the normative acts.

Article 8

Regulations and directives issued by the Commission are binding upon financial and capital market participants. Regulations are effective as of the day following their publication in the government journal Latvijas Vestnesis, if same regulations do not provide for otherwise.

Article 9

The Commission shall be responsible for:

    1) stability and development of the financial market;

    2) promotion of free competition within the financial market.

Section III

Relation of the Commission with the Bank of Latvia and the Ministry of Finance

Article 10

(1) At least once per quarter the Commission shall submit information summary on the situation in the financial and capital market to the Bank of Latvia and the Ministry of Finance.

(2) Of short-term liquidity problems of a particular financial and capital market participant or its potential or actual insolvency, the Commission shall inform the Governor of the Bank of Latvia and the Minister of Finance in writing. The Commission shall be authorised to request the Bank of Latvia to extend a loan against collateral to any such credit institution.

(3) The Commission and Bank of Latvia shall share the statistic relevant to execution of their tasks.

Article 11

The Commission shall provide information on the financial status of specific credit-institutions upon a written request of the Governor of the Bank of Latvia.

Article 12

If not otherwise specified by regulatory requirements, the information referred to in this Section shall be considered restricted.

Section IV

Establishment and Management of the Commission

Article 13

(1) The Commission shall be governed by its Council.

(2) The Council shall be comprised of five members: the Chairperson of the Commission (hereinafter, Chairperson), his/her Deputy and three members, who are also directors of the Commission's Departments.

(3) The Parliament shall appoint the Chairperson and his/her Deputy for a period of six years upon a joint proposal of the Minister of Finance and the Governor of the Bank of Latvia.

(4) The Chairperson shall appoint and remove other members of the Council coordinating his/her decision with the Governor of the Bank of Latvia and the Minister of Finance.

(5) A person may be appointed to the position of Chairperson, Deputy Chairperson or a Council member provided that he/she:

1) is competent in financial management;

2) is of good repute;

3) has at least five years experience in the financial and capital market.

(6) The position of Chairperson, Deputy Chairperson or Council member shall not be taken by a person who:

1) has a criminal record for committing a deliberate offence, irrespective of its annulment or removal;

2) has been deprived of the right to engage in a particular or any type of entrepreneurial activity.

Article 14

The Parliament shall dismiss the Chairperson or Deputy Chairperson from his/her position before the end of their terms as specified under Paragraph 2 of Article 13 only if:

1) an application on resignation is submitted by the respective person;

2) a court judgement whereby the Chairperson or his/her Deputy is convicted of criminal offence becomes effective;

3) the Chairperson or Deputy Chairperson is not able to officiate for a period of six consecutive months due to illness or for any other reason;

4) an application submitted jointly by the Governor of the Bank of Latvia and the Minister of Finance, on his/her early dismissal has been received.

Article 15

(1) The meeting of the Council shall be convened and presided over by the Chairperson or, during his/her absence, by the Deputy Chairperson.

(2) The Council shall be considered competent if no fewer than four of its members are present at a meeting, provided that one of them is the Chairperson or Deputy Chairperson.

(3) Each member of the Council shall have the right to call a meeting of the Council by submitting a written application.

(4) Meeting of the Council shall be convened on an as-needed basis, however, not less frequently than once a month.

Article 16

(1) The Council shall pass resolutions by a simple majority. In case of vote parity, the vote of the chairperson of the meeting shall be decisive.

(2) The Governor or Deputy Governor of the Bank of Latvia and the Minister of Finance may participate in Council meetings in the capacity of advisors. Heads of the public organizations (professional associations) of financial and capital market participants may also take part in Council meetings in such capacity, provided that these meetings have not been declared closed by a resolution of the Council.

(3) All Council members attending a Council meeting shall sign its minutes.

(4) If any Council member does not agree with a resolution of the Council and votes against it, his/her individual opinion shall be recorded in the minutes and he/she shall not be held responsible for this resolution of the Council.

Article 17

The Council shall have the exclusive right:

1) to approve supervisory and regulatory policies for the financial and capital market;

2) to issue binding regulations and directives regulating activities of financial and capital market participants;

3) to issue special permits (licenses) or certificates authorising operation in the financial and capital market;

4) to suspend and renew the validity of the special permits (licenses) or certificates issued;

5) to annul any special permit (license) or certificate issued;

6) to take decisions on the applications of sanctions against persons in breach of any of the regulatory requirements pertaining to the financial and capital market;

7) to specify payments to be made by financial and capital market participants to finance the activities of the Commission;

8) to approve the structure of the Commission, its Statutes and structural units;

9) to approve the annual budget of the Commission;

10) to establish remuneration for the Commission's staff;

11) to approve the Commission's performance and annual report;

12) to approve the procedure for registration, processing, storage, distribution and liquidation of information at the disposal of the Commission;

13) to pass resolutions on signing cooperation agreements with the Bank of Latvia and foreign financial supervision authorities on the exchange of information necessary for supervision and regulation of the financial and capital market;

Article 18

(1) The Chairperson shall represent the Commission and shall be responsible for the organization of its activity. In the Chairperson's absence, his/her duties shall be performed by the Deputy Chairperson.

(2) The Chairperson shall hire and dismiss the Commission's staff.

(3) The Chairperson shall represent the Commission in its relations with state institutions, financial and capital market participants and international organizations.

Section V

Responsibility of the Officials and Staff of the Commission

Article 19

(1) The members of the Council, heads of its structural units, and other employees are officials of the Commission. The list of the employees to be ranked as government officials shall be approved by the Chairperson;

(2) To determine the restrictions on entrepreneurial activities, gaining income, combining positions and execution of tasks, as well as other related restrictions, duties and responsibilities of the officials of the Commission, the provisions of the Anti-corruption law apply.

Article 20

(1) The Council members as well as heads and employees of the structural units of the Commission are prohibited from publicly disclosing or disseminating in any other manner, both during the their office term, and after termination of their employment or any other contract relationship with the Commission, data or any other information related to financial and capital market participants that has not been previously published in accordance with procedures set by law or whose disclosure has not been approved by the Council.

(2) The persons specified under Clause (1) of this Article, in compliance with the regulatory requirements, shall be held responsible for any illegal disclosure of restricted information as well as for any loss incurred by third parties as a result of unlawful actions of the Commission's employees.

Section VI

Consultative Council of the Financial and Capital Market Commission

Article 21

(1) Consultative Council of the Financial and Capital Market Commission (hereinafter, the Consultative Council) shall be established to promote the efficiency of the monitoring of the financial and capital market and promotion of its safety, stability and growth. It shall be a collegial, advisory body charged with the following tasks:

1) to review legislation drafted for the regulation of activities of financial and capital market participants;

2) upon a financial and capital market participant's request and prior to consideration by the Commission, to review the participant's complaints regarding the findings of the Commission's inspections;

3) to prepare policy recommendations for the Council relevant to the execution of the Commission's functions as set by law, and improvement and development of the financial and capital market regulation and monitoring;

4) to review the Commission's annual budget and issue its opinion thereupon;

5) to submit proposals to the Chairperson of the Commission regarding improvement of the Commission's activities;

6) to supervise the accrual of funds with the Deposits Guarantee Fund and the Fund for the Protection of the Insured and compensation payments from these Funds.

(2) If the Council's decision does not agree with the opinion previously made by the Consultative Council on the same issue, the minutes of the Council meeting shall reflect the motivation for declining said opinion.

(3) The Consultative Council shall be comprised of representatives of the Commission and heads of the public organizations (professional associations) of financial and capital market participants on the principle of parity.

(4) The Consultative Council shall be considered competent if at least half of its members are present at its meeting. It shall pass resolutions by a simple majority of vote of the members present. In case of vote parity, the resolution shall be considered not passed.

(5) The meeting of the Consultative Council shall be presided by the Chairperson or Deputy Chairperson of the Commission.

(6) The Commission shall be responsible for the record keeping of the Consultative Council.

Section VII

Financing of the Commission

Article 22

(1) Activities of the Commission shall be financed from payments of the participants of the financial and capital market made in the amounts specified by the Council and not exceeding the amount set by law. The participants' payments shall be transferred to the Commission's account with the Bank of Latvia and utilized solely for the purpose of financing its activities.

(2) Payments by permanent representative offices and branches of foreign undertakings (business enterprises) engaging in entrepreneurial activity in the Republic of Latvia as participants of the financial and capital market shall be made as provided for under Article 23 of this Law.

Article 23

(1) The Commission's revenue shall be comprised of:

1) insurers' payments calculated from the total sum of the received quarterly insurance premiums:

a) up to 0.4% (inclusive) of life insurance transactions related to the accrual of funds;

b) up to 0.2% (inclusive) of transactions related to the third party mandatory civil liability insurance of land vehicle owners;

c) up to 0.7% (inclusive) of other insurance;

2) private pensions fund payments of up to 0.4% (inclusive) of quarterly contributions made by or on behalf the pension plan members within pension plans licensed by private pension funds;

3) credit institutions' payments of up to 0.033% (inclusive) of the average quarterly value of their assets;

4) brokerage companies' payments of up to 1% (inclusive) of the average quarterly gross income from their transactions, but not less than 2,000 lats per year;

5) Stock Exchange payments of up to 2% (inclusive) of the average quarterly gross income from the Stock Exchange transactions, but not less than 5,000 lats per year;

6) Depository payments of up to 2% (inclusive) of the average quarterly gross income from the Depositor's transactions, but not less than 5,000 lats per year;

7) investment companies' payments of up to 0.033% (inclusive) of the quarterly average asset value of investment funds managed by the investment companies, but not less than 2,500 lats per year;

8) income from services provided by the Commission as set by law;

9) (*) payments of credit unions for financing the activities of the Commission of up to 0.033% of the average quarterly value of their assets.

(2) Payments for financing the Commission are made by each participant in the financial and capital market in compliance with Paragraph 1 of this Article and Paragraph 2 of Article 22.

Article 24

(1) In accordance with the provision and terms set forth by the Commission, financial and capital market participants shall file with the Commission reports as necessary for the calculation of payments determined by Article 23 and make payments for financing the Commission by 30th day of the first month following the end of each quarter.

(2) The Commission shall issue binding regulations on the filing of the reports specified under Paragraph 1 of this Article and on calculation of payments.

(3) The Payments made by financial and capital market participants for financing the Commission shall be accounted for as their expenditure.

Article 25

(1) A delayed or incomplete transfer of payment to the Commission's account with the Bank of Latvia shall incur a penalty in the amount of 0.05% of the outstanding amount per each of delay.

(2) Financial and capital market participants shall transfer the penalty calculated for the delay in payment to the Commission's account with the Bank of Latvia.

Article 26

The end of the year balance of the Commission's accounts with the Bank of Latvia shall remain at the disposal of the Commission and shall be utilized in the succeeding year for financing the budget expenditure approved by the Council.

Section VIII

Control over the Commission's Activity

Article 27

The Commission shall annually—but no later than 1 July—file with the Parliament and the Ministry of Finance a written report on its performance during the proceeding year and full annual accounts audited by a sworn auditor (*).

Article 28

The Commission shall publish its balance sheet statement and the opinion of the sworn auditor in the government journal Latvijas Vestnesis not later than on July 1 following the end of the reporting year.

Transitional Provisions

1. The Credit Institutions Supervision Department of the Bank of Latvia, the Securities Market Commission and the Insurance Supervision Inspectorate shall merge by June 30, 2001.

2. The Commission shall commence its activities on July 1, 2001.

3. The Commission shall be the legal successor of the rights, obligations and liabilities of the Securities Market Commission and the Insurance Supervision Inspectorate, rights pertaining to the management of the Deposits Guarantee Fund, and Bank of Latvia's rights, obligations and liabilities credit institution's supervision.

4. By August 31, 2000 the Chairperson shall set the Commission's draft budget for 2001. The expenses related to the establishment pertaining to the supervision of its activities shall be proportionally covered from the funds of the Bank of Latvia, Securities Market Commission and Insurance Supervision Inspectorate.

5. Within the period from July 1, 2001 to December 31, 2006, activities of the Commission shall be financed from payments made by the participants in the financial and capital market, the state budget and the Bank of Latvia as follows:

   1) expenses related to the supervision of credit institutions:

   a) in the years 2001, 2002 and 2003, 1,200,000 lats shall be provided by the Bank of Latvia;

   b) in the year 2004, 960,000 lats shall be provided by the Bank of Latvia and the rest by credit institutions in compliance with the provisions set out in Section VII hereof;

   c) in the year 2005, 600,000 lats shall be provided by the Bank of Latvia and the rest by credit institutions in compliance with the provisions set out in Section VII hereof;

   d) in the year 2006, 240,000 lats shall be provided by the Bank of Latvia and the rest by credit institutions in compliance with the provisions set out in Section VII hereof;

   2) expenses related to the supervision of insurance shall be covered by the insurers in compliance with the provisions set out in Section VII hereof;

3) (*) expenses related to the supervision of the securities market and private pension funds:

    a) in the year 2001, 100% of the total shall be covered from the state budget;

    b) in the year 2002, 198,962 lats shall be provided by the state budget and 50,000 lats by financial and capital market participants, except credit institutions and insurers, in compliance with the provisions set out in Section VII hereof;

    c) in the year 2003, 150,000 lats shall be provided by the state budget and 100,000 lats by financial and capital market participants, except credit institutions and insurers, in compliance with the provisions set out in Section VII hereof;

    d) in the year 2004, 100,000 lats shall be provided by the state budget and 150,000 lats by financial and capital market participants, except credit institutions and insurers, in compliance with the provisions set out in Section VII hereof;

    e) in the year 2005, 50,000 lats shall be provided by the state budget and 200,000 lats by financial and capital market participants, except credit institutions and insurers, in compliance with the provisions set out in Section VII hereof;

    f) in the year 2006, 250,000 lats shall be provided by financial and capital market participants in compliance with the provisions under Section VII hereof;

(4) (*) expenses related to the supervision of credit unions shall be covered by credit unions in compliance with the provisions set out in Section VII hereof.

6. The payment defined under Paragraph 1 of Article 5 of the Transitional Provisions shall be executed by the Bank of Latvia once per quarter by the 15th day of the first month of each quarter in an amount equal to one fourth of the amount that the Bank of Latvia is due to cover in the respective year.

7. Commencing with the year 2007, the activities of the Commission shall be fully financed from the payments of financial and capital market participants.

8. Licenses (permits) and professional qualification certificates issued by the Securities Market Commission, the Insurance Supervision Inspectorate and the Bank of Latvia for operation in the financial and capital market still valid on July 1, 2001 shall be valid until their expiration. Provisions for intensified supervision and restrictions on financial services applied by the Bank of Latvia in accordance with the Law on Credit Institutions that are effective on July 1, 2001 shall remain valid until the Commission resolves to abolish them.

9. Until the passage of the respective regulatory requirements of the Commission, yet not later than by January 1, 2002, the following Cabinet of Ministers Regulations shall remain effective, unless this law stipulates otherwise:

1) the Cabinet of Ministers Regulation No. 401 of October 6, 1998 for Payments to the Protection Fund of the Insured;

2) the Cabinet of Ministers Regulation No. 421 of October 27, 1998 for the Annual Reports of Insurance Companies;

3) the Cabinet of Ministers Regulation No. 436 of November 17, 1998 for the Registration Rules for Insurance Companies and Insurers;

4) the Cabinet of Ministers Regulation No. 441 of November 24, 1998 for Accounting for Insurance Broker's Services in Insurance Brokerage Companies;

5) the Cabinet of Ministers Regulation No. 442 of November 24, 1998 for Insurance Brokerage Companies Civil Liability Insurance;

6) the Cabinet of Ministers Regulation No. 18 of January 19, 1999 for the Certification of Insurance Brokers;

7) the Cabinet of Ministers Regulation No. 91 of March 17, 1998 for Special Permits (Licenses) for the Operation of Private Pension Fund;

8) the Cabinet of Ministers Regulation No. 234 of July 7, 1998 for the Calculation of Additional Capital Accrued with Private Pension Fund;

9) the Cabinet of Ministers Regulation No. 253 of July 14, 1998 for the Private Pension Fund's Annual Report.

10. until the adoption of the respective regulatory documents by the Commission, but no later than January 1. 2002, binding regulations, issued by the Securities Market Commission, Insurance Supervision Inspectorate and the Bank of Latvia, governing the operation of financial and capital market participants, calculation of their performance indicators and reporting shall remain effective unless this law stipulates otherwise.

11. As of July 1, 2001, the Law on the Securities Market Commission shall be no longer in effect (Zinotajs of the Parliament of the Republic of Latvia and the Cabinet of Ministers, 1995, No. 20; 1997, No. 14; 1998, No. 23).

Select Bibliography

Abrams, R. K. & M. Taylor, *Issues in the Unification of Financial Sector Supervision*, IMF Operational Paper MAE/00/03 (IMF 2000).

Alesina, A. & R. Gatti, *Independent Central Banks: Low Inflation at No Costs*, 85 Amer. Econ. Rev., Papers and Proceedings.

Alexander, W., J. Davis, L. Ebrill & C. J. Lindgren, (eds.) *Systemic Bank Restructuring and Macroeconomic Policy* (IMF 1997).

Arora, A., *Practical Banking and Building Society Law* (Blackstone Press 1997).

Bean, C., *The New UK Monetary Arrangement: A view from the literature*, 108 Econ. J. 1795–1809 (1998).

Bjerre-Nielsen, H., *Objectives, functions and structure of an integrated supervisory authority*, paper presented at a conference on the challenges of unified financial supervision in the new millennium (Tallinn, July 2001).

Blair, M., R. Cranston, C. Ryan & M. Taylor, *Blackstone's Guide to The Bank of England Act 1998* (Blackstone Press Ltd. 1998).

Blake, A. P. & M. Weale, *Costs of Separating Budgetary Policy from Control of Inflation: A Neglected Aspect of Central Bank Independence*, 50 Oxford Economic Papers (1998).

Briault, C. B., *Building a single financial services regulator*, paper presented at a conference on the challenges of unified financial supervision in the new millennium (Tallinn, July 2001).

———, *The Rationale for a Single National Financial Services Regulator*, Occasional Paper Series No. 2 (Financial Services Authority 1999).

———, *A Single Regulator for the UK Financial Services Industry*, Financial Stability Review (November 1998).

Briault, C. B., A. G. Haldane & M. A. King, *Independence and Accountability*, Bank of England Working Paper No. 49 (Bank of England 1996).

Caprio Jr., G. & P. Honohan, *Beyond Capital Ideals: Restoring Banking Stability*, Policy Working Paper 2235 (The World Bank 1999).

Central Banking Publications, *How Countries Supervise their Bank, Insurers and Securities Markets* (Central Banking Publications 1999).

Challenges for the Unified Financial Supervision in the New Millennium (The World Bank and Ministry of Finance of Estonia 2001).

Cranston, R., *Principles of Banking Law* (Clarendon Press 1997).

Da Costa, M., *Book Review of R. de Krivoy, Collapse: The Venezuelan Banking Crisis of '94,* 38(1) Fin. & Dev. J. (2001).

Daemestri, E. & F. Guerrero, *The Rationale for Integrated Financial Services Supervision in Latin America and the Caribbean*, Technical Paper Series IFM-135 (Inter-American Bank 2003).

Daniel, H. & C. Pzarbasioglu, *Leading Indicators of Banking Crises— Was Asia Different?*, Working Paper WP/98/91-EA (IMF 1998).

de Luna Martinez, J., & T. A. Rose, *International Survey of Integrated Financial Sector Supervision*, Financial Sector Operations Policy Department: Policy Research Working Paper No. 3096 (The World Bank 2003).

Debelle, G., *Central Bank Independence: A Free Lunch?*, IMF Working Paper, No. 96/1 (IMF 1996).

Diamond, D. & P. Dybvig, *Bank Runs, Deposit Insurance, and Liquidity*, 91(3) J. Polit. Econ. (1983).

Drees, B. & C. Pazarbasioglu, *The Nordic Banking Crisis: Pitfalls in Financial Liberalization?*, Occasional Paper 161 (IMF 1998).

Dziobek, C. & C. Pazarbasioglu, *Lessons from Systemic Bank Restructuring* (IMF 1998).

Ferran, E., *Examining the UK's Experience in Adopting a Single Financial Regulator Model*, 28 Brook. J. Intl. L. 257 (2003).

Folkerts-Landau, D. & C. Lindgren, *Toward a Framework for Financial Stability* (IMF 1998).

Fuhrer, J. C., (ed.) *Goals, Guidelines, and Constraints Facing Monetary Policy Makers*, Federal Reserve Bank of Boston Conference Series No. 38 (Federal Reserve Bank of Boston 1994).

Goodhart, C. A. E., P. Hartman, D. T. Llewellyn, L. Rojas-Suarez & S. Weisbrod, *Financial Regulation* (Routledge 1998).

Halvorsen, M. G., *Process of Merging Different Supervisory Agencies*, paper presented at a conference on the challenges of unified financial supervision in the new millennium (Tallinn, July 2001).

International Compliance Association, International Diploma in Anti-Money Laundering—Manual (International Compliance Association 2003).

————, International Diploma in Compliance—Manual, (International Compliance Association 2003).

Kawai, Y., *Global Cooperation of Supervision in the Three Financial Sectors*, paper presented at a conference on the challenges of unified financial supervision in the new millennium (Tallinn, July 2001).

Kraft, V. *Safeguarding Financial Stability–Key Issues for the Central Bank*, paper presented at a conference on the challenges of unified financial supervision in the new millennium (Tallinn, July 2001).

Lindgren, C., *Authorities' Roles and Organizational Issues in Systemic Bank Restructuring*, Working Paper WP/97/92-EA (IMF 1997).

Llewellyn, D. T., *The Creation of a Single Financial Regulatory Agency In Estonia: The Global Context*, paper presented at a conference on the challenges of unified financial supervision in the new millennium (Tallinn, July 2001).

————, paper presented at the conference on Regulation and Stability in the Banking Sector, *Some Lessons for Bank Regulation from Recent Cases* (De Nederlandsche Bank, Amsterdam, November 3–5, 1999).

Mehrez, G. & D, Kaufmann, *Transparency, Liberalization, and Banking Crises*, Policy Research Working Paper 2286 (The World Bank 2000).

Mehta, P. S., *Why a Steel Regulator Makes Little Sense*, Business Line, December 17, 2004.

Mwenda, K. K. & D. A. Ailola, (eds.) *Frontiers of Legal Knowledge: Business and Economic Law in Context* (Carolina Academic Press 2003).

Mwenda, K. K. & A. Fleming, *International Developments in the Organizational Structure of Financial Services Supervision: Part II*, 17(1) J. Intl. Banking L. (2002).

————, *International Developments in the Organizational Structure of Financial Services Supervision: Part I*, 16(12) J. Intl. Banking L. (2001).

Mwenda, K. K. & J. M. Mvula, *A Framework for Unified Financial Services Supervision: Lessons from Germany and other European Countries*, 5(1) J. Intl. Banking Reg. (2003).

————, *Unified Financial Services Supervision in Latvia, the United Kingdom and Scandinavian Countries*, 10(1) Murdoch U. Electronic J. L. (2003).

Mwenda, K. K., *Legal Aspects of Unified Financial Services Supervision in Germany*, 4(10) Germ. L. J. (2003).

————, *Unified Financial Services Supervision in Zambia: The Legal and Institutional Frameworks*, 36 Zambia Law Journal (2004).

————, *Unified Financial Services Regulation: The Unfolding Debate*, 1(2) CHIMERA Journal 25–30 (2003).

————, *Integrated Financial Services Supervision in Poland, the UK and the Nordic countries*, 10(2) Tilburg Foreign Law Review (2002).

————, *The Regulatory and Institutional Framework for Unified Financial Services Supervision in the Baltic States*, 9(2) Journal of East European Law (2002).

————, *Zambia's Stock Exchange and Privatization Programme: Corporate Finance Law in Emerging Markets* (The Edwin Mellen Press 2001).

————, *Banking Supervision and Systemic Bank Restructuring: An International and Comparative Legal Perspective* (Cavendish Publishing 2000).

————, *Recent Developments in Banking Supervision and Systemic Bank Restructuring: A Legal Perspective*, 31 Zambia L. J. (1999).

————, *Legal Aspects of Corporate Finance: The Case for an Emerging Stock Market*, unpublished Ph.D. thesis (The University of Warwick 1998).

Posen, A., *Central Bank Independence and Disinflationary Credibility: A Missing Link*, 50 Oxford Economic Papers (1998).

Quintyn, M., & M. W. Taylor, *Should Financial Sector Regulators be Independent?*, Economic Issues 32, (IMF 2004).

Ramirez, S. A., *Depoliticising financial regulation*, 41(2) Wm. & Mary L. Rev. (2000).

Saal, M., *Bank Soundness and Macro-economic Policy* (IMF 1996).

Samiei, H., J. K. Martijn, Z. Kontolemis & L. Bartolini, *United Kingdom: Selected Issues* (IMF 1999).

Sheldon, A., (ed.) *Financial Regulation or Over-regulation* (Institute of Economic Affairs 1988).

Sheng, A., (ed.) *Bank Restructuring: Lessons from the 1980s* (The World Bank 1996).

Sundararajan, L., A. Petersen & G. Sensenbrenner, *Central Bank Reform in the Transition Economies* (IMF 1997).

Svensson, L. E. O., *Inflation Targeting: Implementing and Monitoring Inflation Targets*, 41 Eur. Econ. Rev. 1111-46 (1997).

Taylor, M., *Peak Practice: How To Reform the United Kingdom's Regulatory System* (Centre for the Study of Financial Innovation 1996).

————, *Twin Peaks: A Regulatory Structure for the New Century* (Centre for the Study of Financial Innovation 1995).

Taylor, M. & A. Fleming, *Integrated Financial Supervision: Lessons from Northern European Experience*, Policy Research Working Paper 2223 (The World Bank 1999).

Trink, A., a paper presented at a conference on the challenges of unified financial supervision in the new millennium, *Challenges for Estonian Unified Financial Sector Supervision* (Tallinn, July 2001).

World Bank, The, *Abstracts*, Policy Research Working Paper Series, Numbers 2262–2299 (The World Bank 2000).

————, *Abstracts*, Policy Research Working Paper Series, Numbers 2197–2261 (The World Bank 1999).

Index